SAN FRANCISCO 49ers LEGENDS

The Golden Age of Pro Football

Martin S. Jacobs

Editing by Tex Noel
Layout by Fusion Creative Works
Photos from author's collection

ISBN-13: 978-1532962431
ISBN-10: 1532962436

First Printing: 2016

Printed in U.S.A. by CreateSpace Publishing

Authored by:

Martin S. Jacobs
P.O. Box 22026
San Francisco, CA. 94122

Email: Mjacobs784@aol.com

May the memories of Kezar Stadium and the
49ers of the Golden Age never fade.

Table of Contents

Preface

The 1950s were a wonderful time to be a kid in San Francisco. I was raised by my parents during an age of affluence, also known as the "baby boomer" generation. From dawn to dusk, I enjoyed the good life to the hilt in a new neighborhood called the Sunset District.

The best part of where we lived was Kezar Stadium, the home of the 49ers, located just about two miles away. And when the 49ers played at home on Sundays, the noise from the crowd was like music to a budding 49ers fan's ears.

After Dad returned home from the war, he and Mom bought a two-story Doelger home on 25th Ave. for $6,000, a real bargain in those days. The houses were built right next to one another, but ours had a private backyard with fences separating the property. It was here Dad and I would often toss around the football.

Mom and Dad's idea of relaxation at the end of a long day was sitting on the couch after dinner, reading the evening newspaper or watching game shows on our new 12" screen RCA television, which cost $169.95, from Sears Roebuck & Co.

Dad also enjoyed listening to the 49ers away games on our big Zenith console radio. It was a different story come the start of the regular season, when our favorite team was playing at home. Dad and his friend, Ben, shared ownership in two season tickets, for the six regular season home games the 49ers played. Upon returning home from a game, Dad would always bring me a game program. It wasn't long before he would instill in me his love for the 49ers.

As such, my current collection—all things 49ers—had its beginning. I used my 50-cent weekly allowance, from washing the family automobile or mowing the front lawn, to purchase 10 packs of football cards—each containing 10 cards. I always HOPED at least one pack would contain a 49ers player. Each pack also contained a slab of bubble gum. And, while Mom or Dad subscribed to magazines such as Life, Look, Saturday Evening Post or Reader's Digest, I was able to buy pro football magazines for a dime apiece at McDonald's, a downtown used bookstore on Turk Street.

In the mornings before school, I could hear the foghorns bellowing from the buoys near the Golden Gate Bridge. These sounds were mournful, yet reassuring, as I felt safe lying in my warm bed. A summer-like fog during late Spring would always coincide with the start of the 49ers home exhibition season.

We'd pretty much come and go as we pleased. The most important rule of the day for me, in Mom's words, was "be inside by 6:15 p.m. or when the street lights come on." I could understand why Mom felt so at ease. All she had to do was look out the front window to see where I was.

On weekends, we played tag football games in the street, as traffic was very light in those days, except for a few parked cars. Our games could go on uninterrupted for long periods of time—that is, until the streetlights came on.

If we didn't play tag football, we'd spend an afternoon at Sunset playground on Lawton Street, or at the Polo Field in Golden Gate

Park, for some tackle football without padding. This entailed the garnering of numerous cuts, bruises, and ultimately a few scars.

The field was also where the 49ers opponents would often hold a regular Saturday afternoon practice before their game on Sunday. Sometimes, the opposition would practice at the Kezar Triangle, a grassy patch of lawn outside the west end of Kezar stadium. If we heard any rumors about this, we would ride our bikes there hoping to secure some autographs.

Each August was Dad's vacation time from BOND'S Clothier's in the City. He had dressed San Francisco's society set for decades. It was also the beginning of our annual pilgrimage to Lake County for a two-week vacation at Hoberg's or Siegler's Hot Springs.

Dad really enjoyed driving his 1953 yellow Buick Super. He always made sure we arrived back home in time prior to the start of the 49ers preseason exhibition games, the second Sunday in August. He devoured the 49ers, as it seemed it was all he talked about.

During football season, my friends and I rode our bikes to Kezar, arriving by the end of the third quarter. Once there, it was customary for security to open the exit doors in the fourth quarter.

We would then go inside, hoping to get a glimpse of our favorite 49ers in action, and then wait until the game ended. We then would gather up as many of the rented seat cushions our arms could hold, then redeem them for a nickel apiece. It was a cool way to take home a few dollars for an hour's work.

Soon after, my local grocer told me each Christopher Milk carton contained cut-out coupons for kids under 16 years to see 49ers games for free. Of course, I took advantage of the offer and then had to convince Mom to buy Christopher Milk. It wasn't an easy sell, because Borden Dairy delivered milk to our front door. Eventually, Mom heeded my request.

As years went by, I got a work permit and was hired as a stadium vendor for 49ers home games. I sold everything from peanuts, cotton candy, sodas and popcorn to hot dogs, game programs and souvenirs. The pay wasn't bad either—all cash. We took home 20 percent of what we sold, mostly in quarters, dimes and nickels. Now my 49ers collection would build rapidly with the purchase of more game programs, media guides, photos and trading cards. Regardless of the weather, I never missed a game or a single play while working during the games.

The next best thing to being at a 49ers game was watching the 49ers roller derby team play at Kezar Pavilion in the off-season, on Sundays. The pavilion was located next to the stadium and the matches were broadcast live. It was spontaneous action, especially when they skated against the Rams and Raiders.

In 1958, I attended George Washington High School in the City and joined the sophomore football team. The playing field had a magnificent view of the Golden Gate Bridge and the Marin headlands.

I was a starting halfback and chose No. 39 as my jersey number, the one worn by my favorite 49ers player, Hugh McElhenny. When my number was called to run the "88-loop sweep," I always tried to emulate McElhenny, with his same elusive running style—thus earning myself the nickname "Snake" by my teammates.

By 1960, I was off to college, while always reserving my Sundays for when the 49ers played at Kezar. One thing for sure that would remain constant throughout the decade, my 49ers had always been there like a true friend, with memories to last a lifetime.

Foreword

San Francisco 49ers LEGENDS—The Golden Age of Pro Football tells a story about the 49ers' players my generation read about in the newspapers and listened to on play-by-play radio broadcasts and eventually on television.

In 1950 the 49ers were called mavericks by the media. Some said "they were not big enough or tough enough." Still, they played with class and dignity all the way through, and they left an everlasting impression with our City—one that has never been surpassed, either before or since.

They were coached by Lawrence "Buck" Shaw, called the "Silver Fox," who was a local legend, who gave the team instant credibility, during the Golden Age and turned them into a winner, as well. His team was driven by pride, not dollar signs. They looked at it as performance, not press clippings. They were an adventurous bunch, courageous and exciting risk-taking players. I remember the team was unpredictable and full of action. The style of football they played made for a much different game they play today.

They were generalists, not specialists. Substitutions on the field were scarce, and they often played multiple positions for a full

60-minutes of a game when their number was called, whether they were injury-free or not. Such dedication and loyalty meant sacrifice. Players gave their hearts and soul to the team. Winning wasn't everything to them, it was the will to win that defined them.

When the players started a game, they not only were likely to finish it, they sometimes never got a breather. And when they gave up the ball, they merely took to the opposite side, lining up on defense against the same players who had just been defending against them. They played when, for the most part, no face masks were worn early on and when retaining all of their teeth until the end of the game was seldom realized.

One of the team's most coveted positions was that of playing halfback. Although in order to be considered for the position, a player would have to be capable of not just his normal responsibilities of running, blocking and catching the football, but he was expected to play defense as well. He would have to display the ability to tackle, knock down passes and be in a position to intercept a forward pass. In addition, placekickers and punters would quite often hold another position as well.

Starting quarterback, Frankie Albert, would be called upon to handle the punting responsibilities, while offensive end, Gordy Soltau, would handle the place-kicking chores. The term "specialist" had not entered the list of football definitions until the mid-1950s. Salaries were low (on average $150 per game with no benefits), while most players held "real" jobs, during the off season.

While most of the player's featured in my book are not household names for the current generation of fans, they earned their share of laurels and a place in both San Francisco and NFL lore. They had no shortage of famous personalities, and they were known for their on-field heroics.

The colorful antics of men like halfback Hugh McElhenny, (aka "The King"), one of the greatest open-field runners ever, dazzled the fans during the Golden Age; tackle Leo "The Lion" Nomellini, who perhaps had a disposition better suited for hand-to-hand combat, was no doubt one the most aggressive defensive tackles in the NFL ever; linebacker Hardy "The Hatchet" Brown hammered everything and everybody in sight, with his signature shoulder tackles.

Outstanding quarterbacks who exemplified that fighting spirit were Frankie "The Wizard" Albert, and Y. A. "The Colonel" Tittle. Their magnificent passing and bootlegs, highlighted by Tittle's famed "alley-oop" passes to flanker R. C. Owens, were spectacular. Ends, Billy Wilson and Gordy Soltau, were the cornerstones of the 49ers receiving corps, who became two of the most feared receivers in the NFL.

Matt Hazeltine played 14 straight seasons at the linebacker position, earning himself the nickname "Iron Man;" the versatile Charley Powell was a defensive end, who between stints with the team, was a heavyweight boxing contender who fought Muhammad Ali. He was considered one of the most highly rated, multi-talented athletes of his generation.

In the decade, the 49ers may have assembled one of the greatest backfields ever. They came to be known as the "Million Dollar Backfield," made up of Joe Perry, John Henry Johnson, Tittle and McElhenny—all enshrined in the Pro Football Hall of Fame. They all made great stories to share. These players opened up new frontiers and laid a solid foundation for the championship years to follow.

From their swirling tales of the old AAFC rivalries, and throughout the 1950s decade in the NFL, my book will bring back those memories with each turn of the following pages, as their accomplishments will remain alive, with the deeds and foibles of those who, by their performance, their personality, or both, gave flavor and substance to those times that were as unique in their own right as in their interviews.

For any 49ers' fan that followed this team in the Golden Age, you will find my book not just the story of a football team coming of age but a stirring evocative collection of reminiscences that touches upon what it meant to be a 49ers' fan.

—The Author

Introduction

During the formative years of the 49ers franchise, beginning in 1946, San Franciscans were feeling pretty good about things. The war was over and its citizens continued to bask in the afterglow of V-J Day that heralded the beginning of a new era. Life was getting both sweeter and softer for the urbanites. Personal income rose and new homes were selling faster than they could be built.

The inhabitants of The City by the Bay enjoyed widespread full-time employment. The boom was on in new cars and, of course, babies. La Dolce Vita, the good life that San Franciscans increasingly enjoyed, invited the pursuit of leisure activities, and the local sports were certainly one activity that was flourishing.

San Francisco: becoming a Sports Haven...The Triple-A baseball franchise, the San Francisco Seals of the Pacific Coast League won a record 115 games in 1946, breaking an attendance record in their wake, while basking in admiration amidst free-flowing champagne following winning their fourth Governor's Cup over their rival Hollywood Stars. Joe Verducci's San Francisco State's Gators college football team was fast becoming a Far West powerhouse, in their own right.

The Polytechnic Parrots preps from the inner Sunset District won the City high school football championship before a huge crowd of 41,000 at Kezar Stadium. San Francisco's own Clippers, a pro football team, which was at best a high-level minor league team comprised of college players recruited from the length of the west coast, ended their season with a 6-4 record, good enough for second place in the Pacific Coast Football League. Could sports get any better in our fair City?

A new major league pro football team led by Tony Morabito, a shrewd San Francisco trucking executive described by the press as an "impractical dreamer," nonetheless formed a new franchise dedicated to our growing metropolis.

He and his handpicked investors would put up $250,000 to finish the structuring of the new franchise in time for the first kickoff. He would call the team that would kick off its inaugural season of 1946 the "49ers," as to honor the pioneers of the Gold Rush era. With unbridled enthusiasm, San Franciscans embraced their new tenants and their implied promise to provide the City with fiercely competitive games, new thrills and newly minted sports heroes.

Morabito revitalized a sport that by the end of the decade would be on its way to becoming a new San Francisco obsession. The 49ers not only reflected the spirit of the times but also benefited from the spirit and unwavering support of a new generation of upstart "baby boomer" fans, who were maturing and grappling with their own growing pains in concert with those of the similarly coming-of-age 49ers.

In retrospect, while the generation of "boomers" was evolving for better or for worse, as a sport, football was the only one that arguably changed for the better throughout the years.

The 49ers were the first members of the new All-America Football Conference (AAFC, 1946-49), playing with outstanding first-year players, like quarterback Frankie Albert; halfbacks Joe Ventrano, Ken Casenega, and Johnny Strzykalski; ends Alyn Beals and Ed Balatti; guard Visco Grgich; fullback Joe Perry; and coach James Lawson.

These players had gained valuable playing experience playing for armed forces' teams during the WW II era. While other outstanding players came from being members of other NFL franchises: Bruno Banducci, a guard hailing from the Philadelphia Eagles; Norm Standlee, a fullback from the Chicago Bears/US Army; John Woudenberg, a guard from the Pittsburgh Steelers/US Navy; Arthur Elston, a center originating from the Cleveland Rams/US Navy; Len Eshmont, a halfback from the New York Giants/US Navy, and many others fleshed out the team's 32-man roster.

According to Lou Spadia, who then served the 49ers in a variety of capacities, their new head coach Buck Shaw, a respected athletic figure in the Bay Area, would earn an annual salary of $25,000.

The 49es kicked off their first home preseason action on August 30, 1946, against the Chicago Rockets. Playing before 45,000 boisterous fans at Kezar Stadium, the 49ers sent them home happy with a 34-14 triumph. The win caused San Francisco Chronicle sports editor Bill Leiser to proclaim: "Nothing could be finer than to be a Forty Niner! They are the greatest thing to happen to our great City, since the cable car was invented!"

Before entering the NFL in 1950, San Francisco would claim their only AAFC Divisional Championship in 1949, defeating the New York Yankees, 17-7. Offensively, Joe Perry was unstoppable, as he would lead the league in rushing with 783 yards and eight trips into the end zone. Receiver Alyn Beals hauled in 44 passes and 12 scores.

Playing all four years in the AAFC, Albert tossed 88 scoring strikes, a league record. In addition, he was an all-round player, aka a Triple Threat. Because of this ability, his legs served him well; regardless, if he was punting, or his signature run, the bootleg would set-up his passing game. He handled the ball like a magician.

Despite not winning an AAFC championship, the closest Albert would come to winning a title came in the final year of the league's existence in 1949, losing to the Cleveland Browns 21-7—winners of every league championship game.

While not winning a league crown, San Franciscans could rejoice in the fact of a successful four years in the league, at least on the scoreboard. The team would delight all who witnessed their ability to score points. In 54 AAFC games, 49ers fans were rewarded 1,597 points (a 29.59 average). The offensive outburst by the team was a combined 36 more points, registered over the AAFC Champion, Cleveland Browns. The 49ers' defensive unit allowed 928 points, or 17.19 a contest.

After leaving the fledgling AAFC, the 49ers were reshaped and re-created through a series of events that would greatly impact on the future of their organization.

From 1946-49, the 49ers posted a respectable 39-15-2 record in the decade.

1

Indoctrination

I was nine years old in 1952, and it was on a brisk Sunday afternoon in August that my Dad took me to my very first 49ers game at Kezar Stadium for an exhibition contest against the Cardinals from Chicago.

We left our home at 11:30 a.m., and we walked down Lincoln Way towards the stadium. Dad said that this was his weekly ritual, traveling the same way to every home game and back.

The narrow streets leading to Kezar were jammed with cars, many headed in the wrong direction, while fans were coming by foot, by bus, by trolley, even on a bicycles.

We arrived at the stadium around noon. Once there, we stood in a long line to buy two General Admission tickets; mine would cost 50 cents, and Dad's a dollar and 50 cents more. We were surrounded by what Dad called loveable 49er fans—ones wearing overcoats, or leather jackets, red ball caps and wide brim hats. Dad said most of the fans were mostly blue-collar workers, fans coming from a diverse makeup of the City's workforce: mechanics, teamsters and waterfront workers on their day off, or tough guys.

Prior to entering the stadium, I wanted to see the 49ers up close. So Dad and I walked over to the locker room area adjacent to the VIP parking lot, and from there the players emerged from their dressing rooms.

I could hear the sounds of their cleats pounding the pavement below as they headed into an underground tunnel leading to the playing field. My first impression of the players, all decked out in bright red jerseys and silver helmets, was that they looked like gladiators preparing for a colossal battle.

It was at that moment I began to imagine that someday, I would be walking towards that same tunnel, wearing the uniform as a member of the San Francisco 49ers.

We then headed back towards the pedestrian entrance at the east end of Kezar at Williard and Frederick Street, where we handed our tickets to a gateman and entered the stadium.

Once inside the "big bowl," I became aroused. Kezar was now the beat of my heart, and my ears became filled with a deafening sound of boisterous fans that rose into a crescendo.

There was no problem finding a place to sit in the end zone and watch my favorite team take on an NFL rival. We settled on wooden benches, which were about 16 inches per backside, as each row had 36 seats, all numbered. Every 49er would now be playing in front of me.

We sat directly under a giant scoreboard in the end zone. The clock displayed a minute and a second hand, which noted the time left in a quarter, and the score of the game was done manually by a Kezar employee hidden behind the scoreboard.

"When the clock winds down to the final minute, and the two hands converge, the players and coaches have difficulty determining how much time remains, but the referees on the field keep the official time," said Dad.

Game programs cost 25 cents, and Dad was quick to buy me one. Inside the program were great photos of many 49er players in action poses. There was also a cartoon of a gold miner shooting off two pistols, one of which was aimed at his own head! I instantly fell in love with the zany little prospector.

Dad commented that the gold miner shooting his pistols was our official team mascot. Not only did I now get to see the 49ers in person, but I could take that little program home with me and look through it at any time, and revel over my dreams and fantasies of becoming a 49er.

I now could take in the full beauty of the playing field and the fresh green grass, the thick white yard lines and towering goal posts, all which took my breath away.

I can still remember the smell of popcorn in the air and the ice cream vendors chanting, "Yummy, yummy, good for the tummy." If I had wanted a concession item from a vendor, it would have had to have been passed down the row by dozens of fans before it reached me. I settled on "pink popcorn" at the concession stand.

I also noticed the fans were allowed to bring both hard liquor, beer and wine into the stadium. Dad said there were no restrictions, as a Burgermeister beer was available from vendors, who were walking up and down the aisles, for 35 cents a cup.

I was also amused by the barrages of seagulls swooping down and picking up hot dog wrappers and paper cups and then flying off. I believed my Dad when he facetiously told me that when nature called, the seagulls were very well trained and dropped their castings only on the heads of the visiting teams' fans.

Before the kickoff, the armed forces' color guard, preceded by the 49ers' band, came marching onto the field, replete with dozens of majorettes clad in sparkling red and silver outfits, as Clementine, the 49ers' mascot mule, paraded around the stadium.

At 1:00 p.m., the loudspeaker boomed the systematic introductions of the 49ers' players but was immediately nearly swallowed-up with a deafening roar from the fans. I could hear the reverberations bouncing off the stadium walls.

"Good afternoon ladies and gentlemen. This is Dave Scofield, your 49er game announcer," he said. "Welcome to Kezar Stadium for today's game between the San Francisco 49ers and the visiting Chicago Cardinals. And now the starting lineups…"

The players' names were unique as well: Frankie Albert, Bishop Strickland, Bruno Banducci, John Strzykalski, Leo Nomellini, Howie Livingston, Norm Standlee, Gerry Cowhig and Hugh McElhenny. Was that the perfect name for a football player? "Mac-El-henny."

Once the game started, it seemed that all of the fans were either yelling or booing after every play. Some were arguing with each other. Two portly men sitting nearby spent the entire time drinking beer and screaming obscenities at each other.

To say the least, that day back in 1952 marked the beginning of the 49ers having become the center of my cosmos. I became obsessed with the team and never missed a thing that happened on the field.

Over time, I developed a knack for sensing big plays as they unfolded, even anticipating the quarterbacks' play calling, just in time to see a receiver materializing under a deep pass or a runner breaking free for a big gain.

Then destiny intervened!

Something exciting happened on the field that changed my relationship to 49er football forever. It was the second quarter, and my Dad gave me his binoculars to peer through. As I focused my eyes on No. 39, on the jersey of McElhenny, the ball was pitched out to him.

He cut wide to his right and then headed straight up the sidelines, toward the west end of the stadium—all the way for a touchdown! I could clearly see his every move. Not one Cardinals' player laid a hand on him. This play sent the hometown fans into a frenzy. It was a spectacular run!

Later, I would learn that it was McElhenny's first game as a 49er. From then on, the player who would become my favorite of all the 49ers was McElhenny. The 49ers ended up winning the game 38-14, but it didn't really matter to me, as my admiration for McElhenny and the 49ers afforded me a near immortal status in my mind.

I had dreams almost every night of being a 49er player. Once I learned the players' names, I would imagine the texture of a football in my hands, as Albert or Tittle fading back to pass…or watching McElhenny catching a screen pass, as each play would go all the way for a touchdown!

I organized scrapbooks, pasting 49ers' newspaper articles on blank pages, and I contacted the 49ers' team office, as publicity photos of 49er players were free for the asking.

As time passed on, with my perseverance, cupped with good fortune, I built up a massive collection of 49ers collectibles. And today, when I enter my inner sanctum of my home, I am surrounded by a multitude of golden memories—memories that would remain with me, for the rest of my life. And though, I've never met most of the players or staff, I share an unspoken bond with them. But as a fanatical 49er fan, one thing has remained the same throughout the years: I share in my teams' elation and I feel their pain. To me, it's all about loyalty and devotion. I loved going to Kezar. I loved the fans, and I loved the 49ers.

Looking back, it all began when I was a kid sitting in the end zone on that cool summer day in 1952. I'm just so glad that I stuck around all these many years. Maybe it's because life is so filled with repetition and tedium that by comparison, 49er football is so melodramatic. For whatever reason, it's all been worth it.

2

The Debate

Every corner of San Francisco has a story to tell. However, there was one story that I would hear growing up in the 1950s that never seemed to go away, if at all. In fact, the formal debate was between 49ers' faithful San Franciscans and the East Bay communities—as to just who would stake a claim for the San Francisco 49ers football team—that would last throughout the decade.

At the time, everyone knew that the 49ers were San Francisco's own, a homegrown product of Tony Morabito, who founded the team in 1946. But for the years that followed, both San Francisco and the East Bay remained deadlocked over the geographical and athletic harmony of the team. The East Bay claimed it should have partial ownership of the 49ers, and they would not agree that the team solely belonged to our City. They felt our team belonged to the entire Bay Area, but San Franciscans were not buying it.

The East Bay hoped our City would be provoked by its claim of joint ownership, of our civic attitude, which would not lessen the East Bay's insistence the team was of a territory, not as a single city like San Francisco.

"No way," insisted mayor George Christopher. "The 49ers are a San Francisco landmark bred and raised right here!"

Oakland countered that they were on the sunny side of the Bay and were just as concerned with the welfare of the 49ers as the people of San Francisco. "We support The 49ers with word and paid attendance, as ardently as the citizenry of San Francisco," claimed mayor Clifford Rishell of Oakland. "They, the 49ers, are our babies as much as San Francisco's."

"The charge was ridiculous," stated mayor Christopher. Records showed that a couple of years earlier (1954), an article expressing this same sentiment was written under the same request in the Oakland Tribune. That article pointed out Oakland, and environs, had developed an affection for the 49ers, as intense as that existing at the west end of the Bay Bridge.

The East Bay's argument was that everyone called the huge span the Bay Bridge, NOT the San Francisco bridge. Even so, the Bay Bridge, as well as the 49ers, belonged to an area, not a single community was the East Bay's analogy, even to stretch their point to include all Northern California.

To them, the Northern California angle made sense. "Why not confine the 49ers to the Bay Area? Northern California extends from the Oregon border to Fresno. That's a lot of territory, even as the 49ers are a lot of football team," said mayor Rishell. "Anyone doubting our ardent East Bay support inspired by the 49ers has only to cross the Bay Bridge at noon on a Sunday, when the 49ers are playing a tough opponent at Kezar Stadium to an anticipated sellout crowd, and they will see the darnedest traffic jams imaginable created.

"And all those people aren't just going to San Francisco to search for uranium on Twin Peaks or feed peanuts to the monkeys in the zoo. They're on their way to watch a football team that are as much ours as San Francisco's."

Our City wasn't buying it. And though the East Bay newspapers created stories on our team under discussion in their sport's section, they defined our team as "The 49ers," and not "The San Francisco 49ers," or for that fact, "The Oakland 49ers!" It was pure nonsense, as far as our City was concerned.

Provincialism? Civic jealousy in the East Bay? Absolutely. Rather, our mayor once again emphasized the fact the 49ers were solely identified with San Francisco and the East Bay had no sense of ownership. The future did change by the end of the decade, as far as the East Bay was concerned.

Oakland was eventually awarded an American Football League franchise—the Oakland Raiders—following the pullout by the Minneapolis franchise, as it was promised an NFL team. It was our characteristic generosity, and foresight, by our City to share its portion of the region that allowed Oakland to gain a pro football team, while San Francisco continued to call the 49ers its own.

3

The Visionary

Anthony (Tony) J. Morabito grew up in a predominantly Italian North Beach section of San Francisco that bred the DiMaggio brothers, Tony Lazzeri, Angelo "Hank" Luisetti, Gino Cimoli and other aspiring athletes. Although Morabito, nevertheless, was a rabid football fan, principally of Santa Clara University, he learned the game of football in the empty lots of North Beach, and later he had success as a running back at St. Ignatius High School in the outer Sunset District. He went on to play football at Santa Clara, but a shoulder injury during his sophomore season ended his career.

Morabito was the son of an Italian immigrant, who built up a good business in the ship's services on the San Francisco waterfront during the Depression years, only to see most of it waste away. He graduated from Santa Clara University. It was hard times and he was fortunate to get a job as a truck driver for $80 a month.

"I tried to enlist in the Army, but they turned me down because of my partial deafness, which later forced me to wear a hearing aid," said Morabito.

By age 30, Morabito's own initiative, drive and personality carried him from the seat of a truck to a desk, as owner of a lumber-carrying trucking concern, which spread-eagled the Pacific Northwest.

As the country's economy began to improve, so did Morabito's. His lumber yard was in huge demand, as houses were springing up to shelter the fast-growing population that was migrating to the Bay Area. Morabito became a professional football fan after fellow alumni, Nello Falaschi, a fullback for Santa Clara, began playing for the New York Giants.

By 1941, Morabito had become enough of a pro-aficionado to approach the National Football League with a request for a franchise.

It was also the same year a new pro football team, called the San Francisco Bay Packers, members of the Pacific Coast Professional Football League, which was a strong West Coast pro alternative to the NFL, started play in the City.

During Morabito's scheduled meeting with NFL commissioner, Elmer Layden, one of the famous Four Horseman of Notre Dame, the eccentric Morabito got grilled. Layden was not waiting with open arms, and he suggested Morabito stay in the lumber business, where he would be better off.

"Where is this San Francisco anyway?" he wanted to know. "How many people live there?" He talked as if San Francisco was some kind of foreign country.

"Let's face it," as told to the San Francisco Chonicle by Morabito. "The prevalent conception among the NFL was that the West consisted of a vast empty prairie inhabited by cowboys and Indians, adobe houses, and little towns with hard-to-pronounce Spanish names. That's what they thought."

Morabito was shunned, as the NFL turned down his application on two counts: travel to the West Coast was too expensive, and the

Bay Area with six major college teams—Cal, Stanford, Santa Clara, St. Mary's, the University of San Francisco and San Jose State—playing in the vicinity, as well as a new minor league pro football team, the San Francisco Clippers, would soon be starting up in the City.

In addition, during World War II, there would be a host of service league teams created to entertain the troops. Teams like St. Mary's Pre-Flight, El Toro Marines, Fleet City Bluejackets, Second Air Force Blue Bombers, and many others would play their games at Kezar.

Add in the several local high schools to the mix, the City had more football than it could handle. Even though Morabito was rejected repeatedly by the NFL, he was to gain the attention of the football boom that was being played in San Francisco.

At the time, the NFL had only 10 franchises (New York, Brooklyn, Washington, Philadelphia, Pittsburgh, Green Bay, Detroit, Chicago (Bears), Chicago (Cardinals) and Cleveland (Rams)—with just four teams making a profit—and none west of Chicago, and they didn't have any plans to change its geographical structure. San Franciscans only heard through radio broadcasts and rare newspaper articles about these NFL teams, if at all.

Morabito pleaded to the NFL that he could put a team in operation within three months after the end of World War II. It was then Bill Leiser, who at the time was the sports editor of the San Francisco Chronicle, had informed Morabito that Arch Ward, the sports editor of the Chicago Tribune, was in the organizational stages of a new professional football league, the All-America Football Conference.

It goes without saying that Morabito's interest was piqued, and he asked Leiser to make the formal introductions. Ward was truly a sports innovator and had a vision for some of the memorable sporting events of the 20th century, the annual MLB All-Star Game and College Football All-Star Game that pitted the reigning NFL

Champions and the best of the best from the previous season's college ranks.

On June 6, 1944, in St. Louis, D-Day in Europe, Morabito attended the first meeting of the prospective franchise owners of the new conference, and after posting a $20,000 admittance fee, the "Forty Niners" (in the early days, the name was spelled out) and San Francisco were on its way to becoming a charter members of the new league. A curious Arch Ward asked Morabito, "Why the name 'Forty Niners'?"

Said Morabito, adding some historical significance to his reasoning in naming the team: "First, I want to honor them. They were the pioneers who made the perilous voyage around the Cape Horn and poured into the mother lode when gold was discovered in California in 1849. And secondly, it was the Union Pacific "Forty Niner" streamliner train I rode between San Francisco and Chicago, in which I have wonderful memories of. That's why."

By 1946, the country was less than a year removed from World War II and still readjusting. Morabito had two partners when his club began operation in his Lumber Terminals trucking business: Allen Sorell and E. J. Turre. Tony's younger brother, Vic, also had a small investment in the team.

Turre was credited with coming up with the nickname "49ers," and the original team logo was incorporated. The logo depicted a gold miner in boots and in a lumberjack shirt, firing a pair of pistols. As legend has it, the design was taken from a design seen on the side of a railway freight car.

Morabito and his partners, who were involved with the team in its first season, learned their jobs on the fly. John Blackinger, a commanding officer in the Navy, was hired to be general manager. In turn, he hired Lou Spadia, fresh out of the Navy, for $300 a month to be the assistant general manager.

"We conducted business at Tony's lumber yard on Evans Street for the first few months," said Spadia. "We had just four people in the front office, and none of us knew anything about running a pro football team. We were not an instant hit. There wasn't much money in pro football at the time and no drawn-out negotiations.

"The new league did not have a draft the first year, letting teams sign whomever they could," indicated Spadia. "We soon spawned into a bidding war for players with the NFL."

Morabito spent lavishly in his first year, and the 1946 squad was studded with established pros and collegians from Northern California service teams.

"I expect to lose a lot of money on this deal," Tony regretfully said. "I feel it will take time before pro football makes an impact in our City. San Francisco is a great sports town, and I am willing to gamble, but it will take time."

Where admission to a 49ers game was the price of a war bond, only 1,011 season tickets were sold the first season. Morabito went to his alma mater Santa Clara for a head coach, and the silver-haired "Buck" Shaw was his choice.

Persuading Shaw to take the head coaching job of the 49ers was a big step toward insuring the confidence of the public for pro football. Shaw, in turn, hired two assistants: Jim Lawson, who was a star end at Stanford in the 1920s, and Al Ruffo, who played with Shaw at Santa Clara in the 1930s.

Morabito also liked local players from the Bay Area. He signed the popular Frankie Albert, who had starred at Stanford, to play quarterback, and Alyn Beals, an end from Santa Clara. Another outstanding player Morabito had persuaded to head west was Norm Standlee, a fullback, who previously played with the Chicago Bears of the NFL prior to WW II.

Morabito entered into a handshake agreement with fullback Joe Perry, the first African-American, to sign with the club—with a promise of a $5,000 bonus should Perry gain 1,000 or more yards in a single season. Perry got the money in 1953 and 1954, as he became the first of many NFL backs to eclipse the standard that running backs are measured by—1,000 yards rushing in a single season.

Morabito made a futile attempt to sign Heisman Trophy winner Glenn Davis, and Doc Blanchard, who formed Army's famed "Touchdown Twins," to a contract. Although the two stars were entitled to 90-day furloughs, the Army blocked both men from playing pro ball, as cadets were not allowed to play for personal profit during their furloughs.

Then a battle for home turf ensued. St. Mary's, Santa Clara, USF, and the Clippers, who replaced the Packers, played at Kezar on Saturdays and Sundays. The 49ers coveted Kezar for Sunday games and thus were accused of forcing the other teams out. The truth was the colleges and the Clippers were playing to declining crowds. Kezar, which was under control by the Parks and Recreation Committee, awarded the 49ers Sunday home dates. Morabito now had a stronghold in San Francisco.

"We realized that we had our first game coming up on August 24, 1946, and we needed uniforms and equipment for the game," said Spadia. "We also needed to transport the team to San Diego for our first game.

"An army surplus store on Market Street sold Marine Corps duffel bags for $1 each. I bought 40 of them, and they became our equipment bags. A local sporting goods store supplied the uniforms, and my wife's seamstress sewed the numbers on the jerseys.

"Our uniform colors were also tied to local history. Morabito wanted cardinal jerseys and gold pants as a connection to the Gold Rush. But Shaw's wife wanted silver pants, because he was known as 'The Silver Fox.' So the team wore silver pants that first year. But the second year, Morabito decided to go to the gold pants he'd always wanted.

"We played a 14-game schedule, and our league was the first to travel in United DC-3s. We held the bragging rights for a few seasons anyway, because NFL teams still rode trains in 1946."

Unfortunately, both Tony and Vic missed the 49ers' first-ever football game, a 17-7 win over the Los Angeles Dons, before a mere 8,000 in attendance. The owners had planned a Friday morning flight to Chicago for the College All-Star game, and in turn, catch a flight back to the West Coast in time for Saturday's evening opener. Bad weather caused a flight delay, and they ended up in Denver, which in turn, was rerouted to Albuquerque, and then on to Los Angeles where a limousine was waiting.

At 1 a.m., three hours after the final play in San Diego, they landed in Los Angeles. Tony was infuriated about the delays and never paid the pilot the $80 charges, saying, "You didn't fly us over the Rockies, you flew threw them!" The Morabitos arrived in San Diego two hours later and learned by telephone who won the game.

Tony was always a controversial figure, with a "low boiling point." He had a stormy relationship with the press and referred to NFL commissioner Elmer Layden as "incompetent." He once tried to punch Los Angeles Rams' part-owner, Fred Levy Jr., and refused to speak to the Washington Redskins' owner, George Preston Marshall, for years. But he loved his players, and he had great affection for them. The players appreciated Tony's honesty and trusted his every move and word.

"He would come to the practice each day and watch us practice while sitting on a tackling dummy on the sidelines. He never tried to tell his coaches what to do, and he talked encouragingly to his players when he encountered them. At times he would slip players a $100 under the table to show his appreciation for them," Frankie Albert confessed.

Tony loved to live first class. He didn't like guys who put on airs, but he never joined a country club, and he loved to eat in good restaurants.

Two years and a quarter of a million dollars later, he bought out Sorell and Turre. He and Vic became the principal owners, with Tony holding three-fourths of the stock in the team and Vic one-fourth. There was still a matter of putting a team together. Considering he was starting from scratch, he didn't do too bad.

At the end of 1949, it was announced that the AAFC had run its course. The 49ers, Cleveland Browns and Baltimore Colts received an NFL franchise and would begin play in 1950. There was a great shuffling of players back and forth, and when the dust had lifted, only the 49ers had come over from the AAFC intact. From the club-house to the front office, not a change was made as a consequence of the merger.

Tony's first approach to the established NFL: "This is a big country," meaning the Pacific Coast would take its rightful place in the scheme of big league sports. However, when the NFL divisional alignment was drawn up, the 49ers were placed in the National Conference, or the "weaker" division of the revised conferences.

Tony felt the more colorful teams were all in the American Conference. The rest of the National Conference teams were the Los Angeles Rams, Chicago Bears, New York Yankees, Detroit Lions, Green Bay Packers and the Baltimore Colts. With the Rams in Los Angeles,

Tony felt a West Coast rivalry between the two California cities in the same division would generate fan appeal for years to come.

Travel costs were another consideration of joining the NFL. A round-trip air flight from San Francisco to New York was $270. A typical two- or three-week road-trip might include flying to Chicago for a game, then hopping a train to Detroit and Green Bay, or New York and Baltimore.

Travel costs for his 32 players and coaches was more than $10,000, an insurmountable cost to the organization. The Morabitos' losses their first season exceeded $150,000, but they remained optimistic. After a while, Tony no longer had to wonder about the future. In fact, the 49ers led the league in attendance its first three seasons.

"The 49ers will go on forever," claimed Tony. Even then, it would not be until 1957 when Tony recouped his original investment. It was also the year he passed away from a heart attack in the press box, during a game against the Bears.

"Tony Morabito made San Francisco a major league city," wrote Bill Leiser of the Chronicle. "His conviction, passion and character birthed and kept an NFL franchise in San Francisco. He laid the sturdy foundation that has enabled the 49ers to become one of the NFL's premier football powers for years to come."

4

They Also Served

There were 70 former San Francisco 49ers players and coaches who donned a second uniform in either World War II, the Korean conflict or the Cold War. They are true 49ers heroes, whose military accomplishments served our country and performed on the gridiron in the 1950s.

Many transformed their lives, from doing their best in high school or the college gridiron to joining some branch of the military—Army, Air Force, Navy, Marines or Coast Guard. And the majority of them played a vital role in the defeat of Nazi Germany, Imperial Japan, and those who fought in Korea.

They demonstrated courage and sacrifice that was equal of any American forces in any war. Many of them sharpened their skills prior to being discharged, by playing for powerful military football teams.

Below is a composite listing of 49ers players, who also were American Military Heroes:

Norm Standlee, FB (1946-52)*, spent five years in the Army, in which 17 months were part of the China-Burma campaign. He later starred on the Eastern Army All-Stars service team.

Royal (1950) and **Sam** (1949-50,1952) **Cathcart**, HBs. Royal served in the Army Air Force in Europe; Sam was part of the D-Day invasion, fought in the Battle of the Bulge, and received a Silver Star and Purple Heart for bravery in the Colmar Pocket in Southern France, serving in the 75th Division, 291st Infantry.

Joe Arenas, HB, kick returner (1951-57), was wounded at Iwo Jima and was rescued during fierce enemy fire. He spent 20 months in the Marine Corps in the Pacific and received the Purple Heart.

Frankie Albert, QB (1946-52), saw action on a Navy aircraft carrier as a deck officer and spent 15 months in the Pacific theater. He also quarterbacked the St. Mary's Pre-Flight Naval team before signing with the 49ers.

Alyn Beals, E (1946-51), served under General George Patton as an Army captain with the field artillery unit and saw considerable action at Nuremberg, Germany.

Joe Perry, FB (1948-60, 1963), served in the Navy as a coxswain on an LST in the South Pacific.

James "Jim" Lawson, asst. coach (1946-54), tutored the powerful St. Mary's Pre-Flight team before being assigned to duty in the Central Pacific.

Phil Bengston, asst. coach (1951-58), became a Naval lieutenant commander and served on several aircraft carriers in the Pacific.

Howard "Red" Hickey, head coach (1959-63), served in the Navy as a gunnery officer aboard merchant vessels in the Pacific.

Gordy Soltau, E (1950-58), was one of the original Navy "frogmen" and worked for the highly secret OSS (Office of Strategic Services), including swims of up to five miles in the Pacific.

Leo "The Lion" Nomellini, T (1950-63), participated in the invasion of Saipan and Okinawa and played football for the Cherry Point, North Carolina Marines Corps team.

Hardy Brown, LB (1951-55), was a Marine paratrooper during the European campaign.

Arnie Galiffa, QB (1954), received the Bronze Star for wiping out a North Korean machine gun nest with a grenade that observers estimated traveled 75 yards in the air.

George Morris, C (1956), was a first lieutenant in Korea and Japan.

Billy Wilson, E (1951-60), served as a Naval signalman in the South Pacific.

OTHERS IN WORLD WAR II

Navy:
Hamp Tanner, T (1951); Howie Livingston, HB (1950); Rex Berry, DB (1951-56); Lowell Wagner, DB (1949-53, 1955); Bill "Tiger" Johnson, C (1948-56); Bob Downs, G (1951); Visco Grgich, G (1946-52); Norman "Red" Strader, asst. coach and head coach (1952-55); Don Burke, LB (1950-54).

Army:
Al Carapella, T (1951-55); Harold "Hal" Shoener, E (1948-50); Paul Salata, E (1949-50); Johnny "Strike" Strzykalski, HB (1946-52); Marc Duncan, asst. coach (1955-62).

Marines:
Gail Bruce, E (1948-52); Jack Nix, E (1950); Nick Feher, G (1951-54); Harley Dow, G (1950); Pete Wismann, LB (1949-52, 1954).

Air Force:

Bob White, HB (1951-52).

KOREAN CONFLICT

Navy:

Jim Monachino, HB (1951-53); Leo Rucka, C (1956); Bill Jessup, E (1951-52, 54-58); Eldred Kraemer, G (1955).

Army:

Jim Donahue, E (1952); Walt Yowarsky, C (1958); Ted Vaught, E (1953); Julien Spence, HB (1957); Bud Laughlin, FB (1955); Ed Henke, DE (1951-52, 55-60); Bob Toneff, T (1952, 1954-59); Clay Matthews Sr., LB (1950-1953-55); Marion Campbell, T (1954-55); Ed Sharkey, DE (1955-56).

Marines:

Billy Mixon, HB (1954); Art Michalik, G (1953-54); Frank Morze, C (1957-61); Bill Meyers, FB (1955).

Air Force:

Billy Tidwell, HB (1954); Pete Schabarum, HB (1951, 53-54).

OTHERS WHO SERVED IN KOREA

Army:

Frank Cassara, FB (1954); Buck Shaw, head coach (1946-54); Dave Baker, DB (1959-61); Billy Atkins, DB (1958-59); Veryl Lillywhite, HB (1948-51); Tommy Davis, K (1959-65); Fred Bruney, HB

(1953-56); Abe Woodson, DB (1958-64); Larry Barnes, FB (1957); Lou Palatella, G (1955-58); Marv Matusak, LB (1957-58).

Marines:

Henry Schmidt, T (1959-60).

Air Force:

Ted Connolly, G (1954, 56-62); Paul Carr, LB (1955-58).

After serving abroad, some 49ers players were wounded in the war and recovered from their injuries to resume or start their playing careers. They all performed their duty extraordinary well. For the 49ers not mentioned above, please respectively know that your recognition to serving our country is applauded.

* Denotes years with 49ers.

5

Albert's Grinding Camp

St. Mary's College in Moraga, California, served as the 49ers' training headquarters during the dog days of summer. Training camp opened on July 27, 1956, for the coaches and 30 rookies, while the 35 veterans and some walk-ons were scheduled to arrive on August 3 for a grueling seven weeks of training camp.

Head coach Frankie Albert and his assistants checked in two weeks before the rookies showed up, as the veterans reported a week later than rookies. Not attending were a few high draft picks competing at the annual College All-Star Game in Chicago. They included the 49ers No. 1 draft pick, quarterback Earl Morrall, and tackles Bruce Bosely and Bill Herchman.

When Albert got the 49ers job, even his friends feared his dislike of practice routines might be his undoing. Small details were not his style. Only the grand strategy appealed to him. But the sun hadn't yet sunk behind the Moraga hills after the first practice, when those who had him pegged as a "no detail" man knew that they were wrong. The place reeked but not unpleasantly with organization. He had mapped specific sensible work schedules months ago, and they were followed almost to the split second. Things went off like clockwork.

Assistants and players knew what to expect from Albert. He would lecture his players on the importance of conditioning, wanting every man to report for training camp in top physical shape, especially if they expected to win the Western Conference. Albert's philosophy was if they played a game on Sunday, his team should start getting mentally ready on Tuesday, not on Thursday. They had to work up a good hatred, a strong desire, and they couldn't do it on Friday or Saturday. It was too late by then.

"There is nothing as indefinite as success at one of our training camps," quipped Albert. "Too numerous to mention, unknown players from small schools have won jobs from men with all kinds of All-American clippings. Veteran George Maderos was an unheralded collegiate candidate who was our 21st draft pick.

"At the beginning of the 1955 season, he was our starting defensive back, and he has been one of the best players on our team. If eight rookies like Maderos survive this camp, we'll have had a 25 percent turnover of personnel in two years."

The college dormitories where the players resided were neither spacious nor very accommodating. They were perfect for college kids but barely adequate for the pro players. A common room on the second floor of the dormitory was a small room, with a big refrigerator in one corner, some arm chairs and a card table with some open decks on it. The beds were about six feet long and three feet wide.

"When I first got to camp my head hung over one end, my feet hung over the other, and my arms dangled over both sides," said a joshing six foot nine tackle, Bob St. Clair.

At the beginning of camp, players were given complete physical examinations, then a playbook was issued that included training camp rules, which were enforced by the coaches. A typical day could often last from 7 a.m. to 9 p.m.

"Team meetings seemed to go on forever, and staying awake for one after another was a real challenge," said veteran Joe Arenas. "Curfew meant be in bed with lights out at 11 p.m. six nights a week and midnight on Saturday. We had limited sources of entertainment. We looked to each other to help make the grueling days more enjoyable. We told jokes, stories, and guys were just being guys."

A full week of drills began for rookies on Mondays, giving Albert and his assistants time to whip through the tedious schedule designed to separate the "wheat from the chaff," before the veterans joined a week later.

A mandatory breakfast for all players began at 7 a.m., then a two-a-day training session would begin with one two-hour workout in the morning, followed by another in the afternoon. The drills consisted of running laps around the goal posts, conditioning drills, grass drills and wind sprints.

"At my first camp, I remember losing 10 pounds of fluids from a single two-hour practice. I knew this because our training staff weighed us in, before and after practice, to monitor for dehydration," said Leo Nomellini.

A favorite drill of Albert's was the "up-downs drill," in which players would run in place, lifting their knees as high as they could, for 10, 20, sometimes 30 seconds. Then, he would have them repeat another 70 up-downs. No players collapsed from this drill, even during the 90-degree humid weather, and this drill was usually followed by 20-25 wind sprints.

"It was bad enough that training camp took place during the hottest time of the year, but for me, to make their annual pilgrimage from Redwood City to Moraga, where the temperature rose another 25-30 degrees was tough," said Nomellini. "It was an easier drive to Menlo College in Atherton, where we had trained before moving to St. Mary's, and we had better weather to boot. To make matters worse, we had put on an added 20 pounds of equipment while we ran to the point of exhaustion."

After morning drills were completed, about 70 players would gather around Albert, who would then take roll prior to players breaking into five group sections: defensive linemen and defensive backs, with the other three groups being from the offensive side of the ball—the lineman, ends, quarterbacks and backs. Groups were sent the length of the field twice to limber up. Many of the players would carry on conversations as they ran.

The squad would then circle around one of the two captains, Bob St. Clair or Joe Perry, as they directed the calisthenics. They started with stretching exercises, sit-ups, bicycling leg exercises, jumping jacks and pushups. Then the squad headed off to the "ropes," a log grid of roped squares set about a foot off the ground. Players had to hoist their bodies through the course in a series of quick little jumps.

"I can easily say that training camp was one of the most difficult challenges," revealed Billy Wilson. "It would take on the mind and body really severe. After the two-a-day workouts, your body was so bruised and sore that it was nearly impossible to identify a player who wasn't unscathed."

After a water break, the squad would then separate into component parts: the offensive backs, quarterbacks and ends stayed with Red Hickey; the defensive backs moved to an adjacent field with Marc Duncan; the offensive lineman went down to the blocking machines with Bill Johnson; and the defensive linemen headed to an area where they immediately started contact work with Phil Bengston.

"Personally, I was never a big fan of the practice format they had, because guys like us on defense had so many limitations," said St. Clair. "Even tackling the ball carrier in practice was a rare occurrence.

Also, the practice tempo was always a problem. We practiced at one speed, while rookies trying to make the team were going at full speed. The monotony of hitting the same guys every day, for weeks at a time, got monotonous."

Morning drills would end about 11:30 a.m., just before lunch. By 2:30 p.m., players were back on the field for scrimmages lasting 90 minutes, which was preceded a pep talk by Albert along the sidelines, lasting for about 10 minutes.

When he finally shouted, "Let's get started," the players jogged out onto the field to take their positions. The offensive team usually wore scarlet jerseys, while the defensive team wore blue.

"Training camp was a challenge right out of the gate, as you could readily see who came to camp in shape. The offense would perform against one or two basic defenses and play very conservative," added Matt Hazeltine.

"Both sides would concentrate on getting their assignments down. Still, there was a lot of hitting, tackling and trash talking. Of course, this was the main purpose of these scrimmages."

"By the end of the day, your body was so hardened that much of it was no longer discolored from bruising," said Gordy Soltau. "Everything began to feel firmer, but at the same time you were completely exhausted. Trying to balance this conditioning, without wearing down or getting yourself injured, can be a dangerous business."

"As tough as camp was on the body, the mental fatigue was just as real and just as debilitating. While the body was busy colliding with others moving at incredible speeds, the mind was being tasked to memorize the playbook, make split-second decisions, and navigate a social environment that could send some players to the brink of a nervous breakdown," claimed Nomellini.

"The '49ers Gay Review Night' was a welcome break during the long days of training camp. For one evening, the veterans and rookies all together had a grand time. The rookies wore hula skirts and did their best at giving their recitations and improvisations of hula girls. Especially Bruce Bosely. He drew the loudest applauds for his limericks as 'Big Bertha,'" said St. Clair.

Near the end of camp, the coaches would allow the public to attend intra-squad scrimmages. It would be the first public exposure of the team before the exhibition season got underway.

Up to 5,000 spectators would rim the field for the scrimmage. They would cram into the bleachers and along the sidelines, while many stood under the big shady trees. They wore straw hats and came with thermos bottles and sandwich lunches.

After the scrimmage, the crowds would move across the sidelines and gather around the players before they headed to the showers. Some fans wanted autographs, while others would simply walk along with the players for the enjoyment of it.

The kids were the most insistent about the autographs, with the hope of obtaining one of a star player like McElhenny, Perry, Wilson, St. Clair, Nomellini and so many other players who might had stayed after practice.

Throughout the training camp, Albert and his assistants were continually making the cuts to meet the 35-player limit. The rookies were always full of angst, not knowing if they had secured a job. Even the vets who were safe from the ax were still anxious about the loss of certain players they had gotten to know during camp.

On days when cuts were announced, it would mark the end of a close friendship and relationship. They practiced together in hopes of making the team and then must suddenly and abruptly say good-bye.

"I've played in both leagues for a few teams during my stint in the league and have amassed a wealth of experiences and memories from these training camps. It was all worth it," said Tittle.

As with most things in life, training camps has its own set of trials and tribulations. But the rewards and benefits accompanied by these players, during those enduring training camps in Moraga, vastly outweigh the hardships of not making the 35-player roster.

"I know one thing for sure," said Albert. "The 35 players who will open the regular season in September will be 35 guys proud of the fact they're wearing 49ers uniforms and representing the City by the Golden Gate."

6

House of Fanaticism

It has been more than 60 years since the height of Kezar Stadiums' glory days, yet the bitterness and sorrow remain among the 49ers Faithful. Test the pulse of some old 49ers fans, the ones who remember Frankie Albert, Y. A. Tittle, Hugh McElhenny, Leo Nomellini, Joe Perry, Joe Arenas, Bob St. Clair, Charlie Powell, Billy Wilson, Dickey Moegle, R. C. Owens, or Hardy Brown...They all bring their own brand of nostalgia.

Those who loved old Kezar, the memories of stirring competitions against NFL rivals Los Angeles Rams, Chicago Bears, Detroit Lions, Baltimore Colts and Green Bay Packers were brought to life inside its walls.

Kezar was the 49ers' first home where they played for the franchise's first 24 years. Viewed outside the prism of excitement, the stadium was an archaic and tattered one in striking contrast to the stadiums they play in today.

The stadium was designed by Willis Polk & Company and built in 1925 for $300,000. It was a place where the cold bite of the Pacific Ocean would cut right through the fans, chilling them to the bone.

The City-owned stadium was nestled among tall oak trees and next to the infamous Haight-Ashbury District. It was located at Stanyan and Frederick Street, at the southeast end of San Francisco's Golden Gate Park, but with just no parking.

With just a tiny parking lot reserved for VIPs next to the stadium, nearby residents in the area on Stanyan, as well as ones on Willard, Carl, and Arguello Streets, rented out their garages or the front of their homes to make money on parking. On street corners, vendors sold 49ers' programs and souvenirs. Army surplus seat cushions were rented for 30 cents each.

"I was just a kid back then. I got paid a flat $20 to rent out the cushions," said Elmer Carr of San Francisco, "and if they returned them following the game, we'd give them back a nickel off the rental charge. The cushions were rented out of necessity, given those uncomfortable wooden benches inside Kezar.

"If you didn't rent one, you were darn sure to get splinters. At the end of a game, we stored the cushions across the street from the stadium, in the basement of a Victorian house on Frederick."

At the east end of the stadium next to Kezar on Stanyan was a hospital called Park Emergency. Players who sustained minor injuries were taken there by an ambulance from inside the stadium. Those who sustained serious injuries were transported to nearby St. Mary's Hospital, a few blocks north on Stanyan.

Each year during the 1950s, the 49ers opened their exhibition season in August, when the playing field was fresh. The condition didn't last long, because local high schools would also use the field during the week. By mid-season, there would be only dirt and slush between the hash marks and the 20-yard line.

Usually by the fourth quarter of a game, the wispy trailers of foggy weather would roll in from the Pacific Ocean, which became the ultimate fans' stimulant. And when the sun would start setting above the west rim of the stadium, the glare would drive the quarterbacks and the receivers crazy, making it almost impossible to complete a forward pass.

"Kezar was no ordinary stadium. This was my stadium," said St. Clair. "I knew every nook and cranny of it. I played all my high school and college ball there too."

The first 49ers NFL season in 1950, ticket prices to see a game at Kezar were: Reserved Seats $3.75, General Admission $2.00, High School Students $1.00, and Children under 12, 50 cents. A game program was 25 cents; a bottle of beer, 35 cents; hot dogs, 25 cents; peanuts, popcorn or soda,15 cents; and coffee or candy, 10 cents.

Kezar was equipped with every amenity a fan would need, just not enough of them. Because of such, fans would be waiting in long lines for concessions and restrooms. One could miss an entire quarter while waiting to have their respective needs met.

The stadium's two scoreboards were located in the end zones—one at the east end, and another, high above the west end of the stadium. They each were operated manually by a stadium employee. The electric game clock was at the east end of the stadium.

Kids under 16 years of age could sit in the Christopher Milk section in Section "II." For 15 cents, they could buy a quart of Christopher Milk and clip the coupon off the back of the carton to get into a game. But it seemed the age rule was loosely enforced. There were guys sitting in the section old enough to be my Dad, drinking beer or smoking cigarettes. Obviously, they weren't kids.

Sitting in the Christopher Milk section was rewarding for kids. Usually about a half-dozen 49ers' autographed footballs were raffled off during halftime of every 49er home game.

(Author's note: I was one of the lucky ones in 1954, as I won a Wilson "Johnny Lujack" white leather football signed by the whole 49ers' team. I've kept the football in the same box it came in all these years.)

In 1950 the team sold just 1,121 season tickets for their NFL inaugural season, as the 49ers kicked off the regular season against a former AAFC rival, the New York Yankees, on September 17, at Kezar. The 49ers lost its opener 17-7 before 29,000 paid customers.

One thing for sure, Sundays at Kezar were always solemnly reserved for the 49ers' faithful entertaining the masses: Clementine the mascot burro, Joe McTigue's 49ers' band, the baton-twirling Majorettes, stadium vendors, blaring fog and bull horns, and the crowd erupting on a particular play in a roar heard throughout the City.

(Author's note: I recall cowboy star, Hopalong Cassidy, and his wonder horse, Topper, rode into Kezar at halftime. The crowd went wild. He dismounted and Topper was led away. Hoppy walked right into the Christopher Milk section, and for the next 15 minutes he passed out small cartons of milk to everyone, and then exited into the tunnel at the east end of the stadium.)

"Kezar wasn't a bad place, only different," San Francisco Chronicle sports columnist Art Rosenbaum once said. "Kezar was far from ideal, but it brought out the community feeling. There were always a few spots of brilliance, quite a bit of comedy, a great deal of sentiment generated by the underdogs. There was never a dull moment at Kezar."

While the 49ers of the 1950s failed to capture an NFL title, during the early years of Sunday Struggles, they had character. With that, the home team provided a strong essence of uproarious entertainment and a love affair between the 49ers, the stadium, and fans of the City.

The early 49ers faithful knew Kezar as "cardiac alley," as it was where the 49ers' owner and founder, Tony Morabito, took his last breath.

In 1957 alone, Kezar incurred six heart attacks during that season. Many, I'm sure were attributed to when quarterback Tittle and receiver Owens performed the "alley-oop" pass play—a desperation pass usually thrown in the waning moments of the game. The "alley-oop" was easily the most spectacular play during the 49ers' time playing there.

No team provided more thrills during the 1950s than the 49ers. Their outstanding play of many players brought all of this into perspective.

With the procession of three outstanding quarterbacks, Albert to Tittle and John Brodie, other players left lasting impressions as well: halfbacks McElhenny and John Henry Johnson, fullback Perry, and receivers Alyn Beals, Gordy Soltau, Wilson and Clyde Conner. And who could forget the men in the trenches: the likes of Charlie Krueger, Nomellini, St. Clair, Powell, or Browns' devastating knockout tackles.

"There's a lot of nostalgia there," said Owens. "I remember the seagulls. There were always seagulls at one end of the stadium, and as soon as the play went to that end, they all took off to the other end."

The 49ers would host its only NFL playoff game following the 1957 campaign, as they would tie Detroit for the Western Division crown with an identical 8-4 slate. The Lions would win the playoff 31-27 and would be the league's champion that season, claiming a 59-14 over the Cleveland Browns.

Among the many memories of games played inside Kezar, some stand out more than others. For example, a 49ers-Rams game, would bring in an overflow crowd of more than 59,000 delirious fans to this historic structure, while the omnipresent seagulls would retreat to

Frederick Street, along with nearly 500 additional fans who watched the game from nearby rooftops.

"I saw my first 49ers game from those rooftops," said former head coach, George Seifert, "before becoming an usher at Kezar. When Tittle threw those, so high, 'alley-oop' passes to Owens, I felt like I could almost touch the ball."

"49ers fans gave me a standing boo every time we played there," Bears' head coach George Halas said long ago. "I don't mean the people boo louder or longer, but instead there was a special intimacy going on there. When they boo you, you know what they mean. Music, that's what it was to me. Over by the bench was the spot where an irate 49ers fan ran onto the field to take a swing at me, but instead I kicked him in the pants!"

The security at Kezar was operated by Burns Detective Agency, but they were pretty lax. I seldom saw them break up a scuffle in the stands, or for that matter, on the field. The S.F.P.D. from Park Station were usually called in to help get order restored.

During a game in 1953, both the Eagles and 49ers players got into a bench-clearing brawl. No one was seriously injured, though McElhenny, who was in the middle of the turmoil, was taking a risk with his head exposed.

"Once the battle was underway, I wasn't thinking and started winging my helmet at Eagle players," said McElhenny. "I remember about 150 fans coming down from the stands to help us out, but I didn't see any security guards."

Like many of the kids from the Christopher Milk Jr. section, we got into the action on the field during games. When the 49ers lined up for field goals or PATs, we would run onto the field from behind the goal post and try to retrieve the football. The lucky retriever would pass the ball to a group of friends waiting in the stands and run off before we got caught.

(Author's note: During a 49ers-Packers game in 1959, I was on the receiving end of an NFL football from a friend after a PAT.)

The action wasn't always restricted to the field. There was plenty of activity from the fans in the stands, especially at the east end of the stadium leading from the field to the locker rooms.

The tunnel opening cut into the stands, so that 30 feet off the ramp were lined with slopping walls where sometimes irate fans would wait. Sometimes hundreds of them, some cheering the players on, waving programs, while others hurled wadded up paper cups, beer cans or bottles of beer at the players.

Many 49ers players and visiting teams dreaded the close proximity of the rowdy fans. John Brodie was a constant target for fan abuse.

"After a loss, getting to the locker room was a horrific experience," revealed Brodie. "I had to wear a helmet to avoid a dose of beer on my head."

"Coming out of the tunnel, it was really dusty," said St. Clair. "We tried to be the first team out and we'd kick up the dirt. You could hear the other team behind us coughing and gasping. And when we were losing a game, coming out that long tunnel you felt like you were going out to the Roman Coliseum and they were going to feed you to the lions! The 49ers' fans were very passionate and mostly unpredictable."

Ultimately, to restrain the overzealous fans, a chain-linked fence was erected in front of the lower stands, and a cage over the player's tunnel entrance, to protect the players from irate fans.

After the games, most fans were usually too exuberant to remember anything and mingled with the players on the field or were being entertained by the 49ers' band.

The kids too had their moments of affirmation, collecting player's autographs or a player's chin strap as the players headed towards the tunnel.

(Author's note: My first 49ers collectible was a chin strap given to me after a game at Kezar by 49ers' guard Ed Henke.)

The players' lockers were not in the stadium itself but up the tunnel at the east end of the field and beneath Kezar Pavilion's basketball courts. Fans would crowd around the players' locker room or in the parking lot to get a glimpse or a hello, hopefully, from one their favorite 49ers.

One of my fondest memories came prior to a Lions game in 1954. I was 11 years old then, and McElhenny arrived at Kezar in an automobile. Once he parked his car, he started walking towards the locker room and into the assemblage of autograph seekers.

"Can I have your autograph, Mr. McElhenny?" I asked. He took my program, asked my name, and opened it to the picture of himself holding a loaf of Blue Seal bread, and signed it across the ad: "To Marty, My No. 1 Fan." I still have that program today.

A bit of trivia...

Several scenes of the movie Dirty Harry, starring Clint Eastwood, were filmed at Kezar. During the filming, the stadiums' groundskeeper let Andy Robinson, the film's fictional antagonist, live under the grandstand. As a youth, the young actor actually sold programs at the stadium during game days.

That's how it was at the zany old Kezar: cold, crazy, depressing and unforgettable. The 49ers never did win a championship during their long tenure there when it seemed the familiar characteristic chant from the fans were always: "Wait 'til next year!" It was a constant and a fitting reminder for all the melodramatic games played there. For the record, the 49ers' overall win-loss record at Kezar Stadium was 63-30 and one tie during the 1950s decade.

7

T-Formation Wizard

At five nine, 170-pounds, quarterback Frankie Albert didn't look like a football player, but he became the "T-Formation Wizard" and for good reason. Remember, collegiate football in the 1940s era was three yards and a cloud of dust and a time when throwing the football was akin to witchcraft.

And maybe that's why Albert was called the Wizard. He certainly could throw a football. As a southpaw, he could pass, run and kick, and handle the ball like a magician. While in college, he was a nondescript tailback in the Single Wing formation. Under the direction of Stanford coach Clark Shaughnessy, who brought in the T-formation, they went undefeated, beating Nebraska in the Rose Bowl. It was then Albert became known as the "T-Formation Wizard." The ball disappeared more times than a rabbit in a vaudeville show—now you see it, now you don't.

"I guess my ability to handle the ball made me effective," said Albert modestly. "I was pretty good on a bootleg, and I could hide the ball and run it if I had to."

That was his psychological weapon in his arsenal, and improvisation was his middle name.

Through Morabito's faith and head coach Buck Shaw's wisdom, they both believed that Albert was the best player to lead the 49ers in their 1946 inaugural season.

"He might not have had the strongest arm, but he was deadly accurate," said Shaw. "His self-confidence and maturity were un-equaled. He carried an air of poise and articulation unlike other quarterbacks in that era."

Albert was such a popular and influential player with the 49ers that the NFL took notice of his on-the-field merits and considered him the best ball handling quarterback to come out of the AAFC, which included Y. A. Tittle and Otto Graham. Albert was a quarter-back who could always be expected to do the unexpected.

Shaw brought in Jim Lawson, an assistant from Stanford, to help install the T-formation and have Albert run it. Lawson also installed the bootleg play, and he ran it to perfection. Albert would make up plays at any time of a game and anywhere on the field. Most quarter-backs could not get away with this, but Albert knew when to draw the line when it came to Shaw.

On his own, he learned that size and ruggedness were not strictly physical, that there were compensating factors of desire and intel-ligence. And there was overwhelming evidence in favor of his phi-losophy during the 1948 season. Albert would amass outstanding triple-threat numbers, passing for 2,104 yards and 29 touchdowns, adding an additional 1,568 yards on the ground, and he would reach pay dirt 8 more times. And to top it off, his punts averaged an amaz-ing 44.8 yards per kick.

For his outstanding season, he would be beat out Graham as the AAFC's Most Valuable Player.

"Alyn Beals was my main receiver," said Albert. "Boy, did he have some great moves. He was a good faker. I can remember several times setting up to pass and watching the defensive back fall down after Alyn put a fake on him. The back would trip over his own feet. I'd look at the defensive man lying on his butt, while Alyn was wide open."

The 1950 season proved to be Albert's most frustrating season. The 49ers ended up at 3-9 and in the cellar of the Western Conference. Yet an analysis of the 12 games played shows another four or five games were missed by a few points, or for that fact, a few inches.

"Everything seemed to go against us, but we never threw in the towel. Most of us couldn't wait for the next season," declared Albert.

Albert mixed it up on defense as well. Against the Browns and Graham, you could generally find Albert in the defensive secondary.

"I enjoyed playing defense," he said. "I didn't do it as often as I would have liked, but I played back there in some of the important games. When we played Cleveland, it was like the Stanford-Cal game. It was a real big rivalry. Whenever we beat them, it was a big thrill for me."

Albert had one of the best games of his career against the Browns. The year was 1949 and San Francisco was on a roll. They had won four of their first five games and averaged 35 points per contest.

When the 49ers battled Cleveland at Kezar, Albert could do no wrong. He threw five touchdown passes as the 49ers whipped the Browns 56-28. Albert had a successful season, passing for 1,767 yards and 14 touchdowns, while rushing for 272 yards and scoring three touchdowns. He also was selected to the Pro Bowl.

In January of 1951, the Colts' franchise disbanded and all their players were placed in the regular NFL draft pool. A coin flip ensued with the Packers, Redskins and 49ers all finishing with 3-9 records. Luckily, GM Lou Spadia was victorious and the 49ers chose quarterback Y. A. Tittle.

Now Albert would have to compete with Tittle, who had gained critical acclaim during his reign with Baltimore. The two quarterbacks would alternate games during the 1951 and 1952 seasons.

"When Tittle arrived, there was quite a rivalry for the quarterback position," Albert said. "Of course, he was already an established star. I guess you could say there was a quarterback controversy."

On November 2, 1952, the Chicago Bears claim they wrecked the 49ers' team and season. Known as the "The Folly on Fourth Down," the undefeated 49ers (5-0) held a slim 17-10 lead in the fourth quarter.

The 49ers were on their own 32-yard line, and it was fourth and two when Albert would call his own number. Instead of punting, he was stopped short of the needed yardage to keep the drive alive.

From there, the fired-up Bears drove in for the tying touchdown; following the PAT, they tied the score. The scoreboard clock displayed just a minute left in the game when the Bears' kicker split the uprights from 48-yards away to shatter the 49ers' season, 20-17.

After the debacle, the 49ers hit the skids, losing four of their final six games, finishing with a 7-5 mark and in third place.

The end of a Legend...Albert would make his final appearance in a 49ers' uniform at season's end, as he announced his retirement. In his three seasons in the NFL, Albert would put up some very credible numbers. He threw for 10,795 yards and passed for 115 touchdowns, and rushed for 505 yards and scored 7 touchdowns.

After sitting out the 1954 season, Albert was ready to play again. "I was just getting into the car business," he said, "and it was a little slow at first. The Calgary Stampeders in the Canadian Football League offered me more money than I ever made in the NFL, so I went up there for a year. We played two games a week, one on a Saturday, and one on Monday. That was because the farmers would come to town on the weekends. They'd get drunk, go to the games and raise hell."

Albert returned to the States and was made an assistant coach of the 49ers in 1955 under head coach Red Strader. The team floundered under Strader, and Albert was thrown into the fire the next year when he was made the head coach.

8

Bloodlines

Clay Mathews Sr., six foot three, 225 pounds, played for the 49ers in 1950 and from 1953-55 during his tenure in San Francisco. His teammates and opponents alike described him as an outstanding defensive end. He became the starting offensive and defensive tackle in his rookie season when players played on both sides of the ball for a full 60 minutes.

"I had Bruno Banducci on one side of me and Alyn Beals on the other side, and Bill Johnson was the center," said Mathews.

"In 1945, I received a full scholarship to Georgia Tech. I played all four years making All-South Eastern Conference each year," stated Matthews. "I also competed on the swimming and diving teams, and my specialty was the 100 and 200 freestyle. Besides football and swimming, I wrestled and boxed, winning 28 wrestling bouts, losing the first one and winning the next 27, and twice was crowned the heavyweight wrestling champion of the SEC. As an amateur boxer, I knocked out 15 guys in the first round. But I was enamored with football, and in 1949 I was drafted in the 25th round by the Rams, but I was immediately traded to the 49ers."

In 1951, the Korean War interrupted Mathews' football career with the 49ers. "For the next two years, I became an Army paratrooper with the 82nd Airborne Division, and I made a total of 18 jumps, in which 17 of them I needed to be pushed," chuckled Mathews.

"I resumed playing for the 49ers as a defensive end in 1953. I was elected 49ers team captain in 1955 and I had a good season, but the 49ers were going through all kinds of turmoil and strife. Their only head coach since the franchise was formed in 1946, Buck Shaw, was let go. In came a strict Red Strader and changes were made. With McElhenny hobbling, we ended up with a disappointing 4-8 season. Strader was fired, and I was dealt in the off season to the Eagles. I think I could've played another decade, but I didn't want to start over in Philly. I was making $7,000 a season and I had two kids, but I decided to call it a career instead."

There is no telling how his career would have turned out if he had remained in the NFL, although the bloodline qualities and traits Matthews Sr. possessed were also passed on to his two sons.

Clay Jr. was an All-American at Georgia Tech and played 19 seasons with Cleveland and Atlanta (1978-96), for a total of 278 games (third most in NFL history). His brother Bruce was a first-round pick of the Houston Oilers in 1983 and played all offensive line positions (guard, center and tackle). He was selected to an NFL record 14 Pro Bowls and entered the Pro Football Hall of Fame in 2003 in his first year of eligibility.

Jake Matthews is the seventh Matthews to play in the NFL, following Clay Sr. (grandfather), father and uncle (Bruce and Clay Jr.), brother (Kevin, a center with Carolina) and two cousins (Clay III, a linebacker with the Green Bay and his brother Casey, a linebacker with Minnesota).

The Matthewses appear to be a dynasty in the making. The Mings ruled China for nearly three centuries, but they didn't put up these kinds of numbers: 58 seasons, nearly 800 games and 22 Pro Bowls. The Matthewses give you quality and quantity. They are indeed the first family of pro football.

9

Indestructible

When you think of the greatest defensive tackle during the 1950s, the first name that comes to mind is that of Leo "The Lion" Nomellini. Known to his teammates as indestructible, he was six foot three and 260 pounds. He never missed a game for the 49ers from the day he first played in 1950 for San Francisco.

He played in 174 straight regular season games, 60 of which he played both ways on offense and defense, taking only timeouts between quarters and at the halftime intermission. In addition, he played in 77 preseason games and in 10 Pro Bowls, with the latter a team record. Nomellini was also duly recognized as the NFL's all-time greatest defensive tackle in the decade.

He had everything needed to be an all-time pro great: size, speed, agility, aggressiveness, dedication, superb conditioning and the willingness to play the full 60 minutes a game. He knew what it meant to work hard once he hit the gridiron. A four-year starter and two-time All-American at Minnesota, Nomellini was the very first draft choice in San Francisco 49er history.

He was born June 14, 1924, in Lucca, Italy. He came to the U.S. with his parents at age four. His family settled in Chicago. Nomellini did not play high school sports, as he enlisted in the Marines and was stationed at Cherry Point, North Carolina. It was there a Navy pilot suggested he should try out for the base football team.

He did and would play in a half-a-dozen games prior to being shipped overseas. During World War II, he saw active duty with the Marines in the invasion of Saipan and Okinawa. After the war, he enrolled at the University of Minnesota as a 22-year-old freshman in 1946.

"I didn't even get an athletic scholarship," said Nomellini. "I went there on my GI Bill of Rights."

Nomellini was a four-year starter in college, and he played tackle on both offense and defense. He was by consensus All-American in 1948 and 1949. Though the trend already was for two-platoon football, it wasn't a surprise when he continued doing it with the 49ers.

He also wrestled at Minnesota and won the Big 10 heavyweight championship. He was on the track team as a shot-putter and anchored his 440-yard relay team. Nomellini claims to have run the 100-yard dash in 10.6 seconds at age 18, and in college and the pros he often ran down quarterbacks and sometimes running backs behind the line. He was big, quick, fast, aggressive, and thus, he was given a nickname, "The Lion."

In the 15th annual NFL draft (1950), Nomellini was selected by the 49ers with the 11th overall pick. One other player with Minnesota ties, and familiar to the fans, was the 14th pick of the round, Harry "Bud" Grant. He played basketball for the Los Angeles Lakers (NBA), football for the Philadelphia Eagles (NFL) and the Blue Bombers (CFL), and he became the head coach of the Minnesota Vikings (NFL) for 18 seasons.

Nomellini and Grant were teammates at the University of Minnesota as was another teammate, center Clayton Tonnemaker, thus giving the school three players taken in the opening round of the 1950 NFL draft.

At first, Nomellini was reluctant in joining the 49ers, but over time he came to treasure his association with San Francisco.

"I was going to the Chicago Rockets because they offered me $14,000, which was a lot of money in those days for four months of work. I didn't even talk to the Rams, because I knew they wouldn't offer that much," he said.

Then the AAFC folded. His draft rights were assigned to the 49ers, who had been brought into the NFL, and they offered him $8,500, take it or leave it. Nomellini took it. "I wasn't happy at the time," he said, "but it worked out."

Nomellini played both ways—offensive and defensive tackle—for his first five years, from 1950 to 1954.

"I liked defense better. It seemed that defensive linemen got more attention than offensive linemen. I tell you, it was difficult sometimes to stand out there and watch the other 21 players run on and off the field. I never had much time to rest. In fact, the only rest I got was when the other people were changing over from offense to defense.

"One season I was All-NFL on both offense and defense, and I asked the 49ers for a $1,000 bonus. They offered me $500. I said I'd just keep wrestling, but when they offered $750, I reported because I wanted to play football," he said.

With the 49ers struggling to find another tackle, they signed Bob St. Clair in 1955. He fit right in with the team. Now, Nomellini only had to play the defensive tackle position—the position he held for the next eight years. He used techniques he learned as an off-season wrestler to manhandle opposing linemen who often double- and triple-teamed him.

On the line of scrimmage, he was a picture of intimidation. His crew cut and jutting jaw fit snugly inside a 49er helmet. His frightening scowl revealed his missing teeth, and he exhaled grunts and groans that struck fear in opposing linemen. He was a unanimous All-Pro choice six times.

He recalled those early 49er days. "I had some great teammates with the 49ers. There were so many outstanding players—Perry, Tittle, St. Clair, Wilson. I went through 22 roommates on that team. Everyone was a joy.

"We considered ourselves pioneers back then. We went on road-trips back East that lasted 17-21 days. We'd play in Chicago, Detroit, Green Bay, and stayed back there the whole time.

"It was tough being away from the family and friends for so long. We'd practice every day, have team meetings and maybe go to a show at night, nothing out of the ordinary.

"The trips themselves took forever. We flew on props. It would take about 20 hours to fly back from New York. The league was just starting to grow, and NFL football was gaining popularity. I was just happy to be part of the sport. It's grown quite a bit since those days."

Though Nomellini holds the record for consecutive games as a 49er, he said there was one game he will never forget, and it stands out for the wrong reason.

"I most remember the 1957 playoff game against the Lions. That game really hurt. We should have done better. Some way or another, they just caught us. There was no letdown or anything. We were just ahead and blew it," he said. "We were out in front 27-7 in the third quarter, and we felt sure we would win the Conference. Even our fans were leaving Kezar early to celebrate. We were told at the half that championship tickets were being printed up, but the Lions rallied and beat us 31-27. It was a lousy feeling."

Nomellini always said he made more money wrestling than he did per season in the NFL. In 1955, he got his affirmation as a champion wrestler when he fought Lou Thesz for the undisputed National Wrestling Alliance Heavyweight Championship of the World. The match was held at the Cow Palace in San Francisco, and he won by disqualification in the third fall of an even match before over 12,000 fans. Nomellini was proclaimed the new champion.

"I held the title for just four months," he said. "Then I lost it in a rematch with Thesz in St. Louis."

Nomellini's wrestling accomplishments:

1-time NWA World Heavyweight Champion defeating Lou Thesz

1-time AWA World Tag Team Champion with Wilbur Snyder

3-time NWA World Tag Team Champion with Verne Gagne twice and Butch Levy once

4-time NWA World Tag Team Champion with Hombre Montana once, Enrique Torres thrice, and Rocky Brown once

10

Simply "The King"

After arriving just 48 hours earlier, Hugh McElhenny, having participated in the annual College All-Star Game in Chicago, was ready for some action in a preseason game against the Chicago Cardinals.

In less than 24 hours, he was already in a 49ers' uniform, despite knowing only a handful of plays and a few of his new teammates.

On the field, the 49ers were protecting a secure lead in the third quarter. Quarterback Frankie Albert called timeout and wandered over to suggest that Coach Buck Shaw put in the rookie.

"He doesn't know the plays," Shaw observed.

Albert insisted and the coach relented. The 49ers were on the Cardinals 42-yard line. In the huddle, Albert knelt down and diagrammed a play on the ground with his index finger.

"Swing to the right," he instructed the rookie, "and take a pitch out."

"I did," remembered McElhenny, "and I ran it up the sidelines 58 yards for a touchdown."

Albert, who finished his career as a 49ers' quarterback and punter in 1952, may have been the key figure in the 49ers' decision to draft McElhenny.

He got a good look at him while playing with the Hawaiian All-Stars at the Hula Bowl in Hawaii. McElhenny was working out with the College All-Stars, and after watching him, Albert put a call to Shaw.

"I told Shaw, he is really something, he's that good." Albert made his point and the 49ers took McElhenny in the first round of the NFL draft.

At six foot one, 205 pounds, McElhenny began his professional career in the era of high-top cleats and helmets without face masks, a forerunner of the modern game. He was an offensive specialist, who rested when the defense was on the field. In fact, since his specialty was a broken-field run, he was employed in ways that actually minimized his number of carries from scrimmage. As a result of his outstanding play during the 1952 season, he would be named the NFL's Rookie of the Year.

His 684 rushing yards (on 98 carries and at a 7.0 clip) ranked him in the top 10 in that category. In addition, he ran for 94 yards on a play from scrimmage and also ran back a punt 94 yards—both for scores and the longest by any NFL player that season. And for good measure, he would haul in 26 passes for another 367 yards, finishing the season with 10 total trips into the end zone. He was voted All-Pro, and he was selected to play in the Pro Bowl (the first of his six appearances).

"If I had 15 carries a game, that was something," McElhenny said.

Instead, his quarterbacks and coaches schemed to free him into the open field. He took handoffs, pitchouts and screen passes, any play that would turn him loose and up the field. Oftentimes, his numbers were not all that impressive, but after adding in his total yards, McElhenny would reign as the NFL's most dominant offensive force during the 1950s.

His classic running style made him a No. 1 draft pick in the high-profile mold of the running backs in 1952. He came to the 49ers as the ninth overall player selected in the first round and signed for $7,000, while having come down from his initial demand of $30,000.

Albert then introduced McElhenny to his new teammates by saying, "I want you to meet the only man who took a cut in pay to become a professional."

When McElhenny joined the 49ers in 1952, it was questionable whether their franchise could survive financially. He removed all doubts. And that is why he was called the franchise saver.

Tittle said of him: "McElhenny was the greatest broken-field runner I ever saw. His cutbacks were high-strung as a Triple Crown thoroughbred and as thrilling to behold."

No sentence, maybe no paragraph, has ever has been written that describes the full range of his ability to carry a football. He regarded his ability as something of a mystery. He had been a high school All-American at Washington Prep in Los Angeles in 1947, winning the state high school high hurdles championship and setting a national record of 14.0.

Speed? His 100-yard dash had been timed in 9.6 seconds—faster than the Pacific Coast Conference sprint champion at that time.

"Speed is one ingredient," said McElhenny. "I had pretty good speed, but I couldn't beat Perry in the 50. I could beat him in the 100 though."

In 1948, he enrolled at Compton JC (the alma mater of Perry) as he would earn All-American laurels while leading his school to a 48-14 Junior Rose Bowl triumph over Duluth Junior College. Soon after, he was recruited by more than 60 four-year schools.

"UCLA, Notre Dame, Alabama, Washington, Oregon, even the U.S. Naval Academy," he recalled. "The best schools in the country wanted me."

McElhenny chose Washington over all the alternative offers, he said, for a most practical reason. "I wanted to marry my childhood sweetheart, Peggy, and by going to Washington, I knew I could afford to support her."

At Washington, McElhenny set rushing records from 1949-1951 that would stand for decades. His most famous memorable performance occurred in the 1950 Apple Cup game against Washington State. On just 20 carries, he ran for 296 yards and five touchdowns, an average of 14.8 yards per attempt. For the season, he would once again earn an All-American citation, finishing with 1,107 yards. He would eventually play in four prestigious college all-star games—the Shriner's East-West game, Hula Bowl, Senior Bowl and College All-Star game.

"To be a good running back, well, it's just God's gift. It's not something you can teach. I did things by instinct. Running, balance, all of it was instinct. You also have to know where other people are in the field."

But there is something undefinable that the great backs possess. The intuitive cutbacks and changes of direction that were McElhenny's trademark are something that can't be programmed. He related it to a dark alley late at night, danger lurking behind unseen corners.

"You've been down it during the day," he said. "You know where the inlets are, where somebody might be hiding. It's just like a football play; you know where your blockers are. You just try to find them."

Doing that took McElhenny in directions dictated solely by fear ("You don't teach that," he said), and occasionally by just pride. He generally didn't like to compare the modern players with those of his era, because he disagreed with the argument that today's players are better athletes.

"His ability to evade tacklers," said Los Angeles Rams' coach Hampton Pool, "was as great as you'll ever see. He would scare you half to death. He was a frightening thing to witness, believe me, when you were playing on the other side."

Pool remembered once when McElhenny caught a screen pass and cut back against the grain, shedding tacklers in route to a 71-yard touchdown run. In watching the film of the game, he noted that 9 of the 11 Rams' defenders had their hands on him, but none could drop him.

Rams' defensive back, Don Paul, remembered how his team prepared for their arch rivals. "We'd work first on the 49ers' receivers in Billy Wilson and Gordy Soltau, but our number one concern was McElhenny. Once we'd discussed how we'd try to stop him, we'd deal with the rest."

Cursing McElhenny was common among defenders, such as Detroit's Joe Schmidt and Yale Lary: "He'd come at you with power, plus that classic style, raising his legs, give you the shoulder, take a leg away..."

"We were in Chicago playing the Bears in 1952," McElhenny recalled. "I scored three touchdowns and two of them were called back. It was the first time we beat them in two years at Wrigley Field. As I entered the locker room afterward, Albert was elated over the game and stood up and said, 'Perry, you're still "The Jet." But McElhenny's "The King!"' He threw me the game ball and said, 'You're now The King of the halfbacks.'"

The nickname stuck. That's when the legend was born. "The King" was finally coronated. Everywhere he went, defenses devised plans to stop him. Some devised ways to cripple him. They didn't want to just tackle him, they wanted him out of the lineup.

During the 1950s, McElhenny was secure in his reign as "The King," for the same reason that Elvis Presley had become king of rock and roll in the same era, because he electrified the fans, as no one had before.

McElhenny said he didn't remember all his plays, but the "49-pitch-on-two and you just go" was one of them. "I guess I was pretty well known for making screen plays work. The '31-F, 35-F' I vaguely remember was my call for the screen pass."

In 1954, the 49ers and McElhenny were on their way to an exceptional season when he separated his shoulder against the Bears.

The Bears had one of those fierce defenses. Still, his teammates couldn't take up the slack. With McElhenny out of action, they lost three straight games and finished 7-4-1. Even then, that season still evoked good memories for McElhenny because it was the first year the "Million Dollar Backfield" played together.

"That was one hell of a backfield," he said. "Even with all that talent, we could never quite win it. We had an injury here, an injury there. In 1954 alone, we had nine starters injured.

"Y. A., Perry and Johnson were exceptional guys to play with. They were such outstanding team players. I don't know how many times they laid blocks that sprang me. I'm just proud to say I was in the same backfield with them.

"If I had to pick out one opposing player that I never looked forward to playing against, it was Chuck Bednarik of the Eagles. Except for our own Hardy Brown, Bednarik's ferociousness was vicious. He was one helluva player," he said.

In his eight seasons with the 49ers, McElhenny never gained 1,000 yards a season. The reason is simple, as he took very few direct handoffs.

The 1956 season was his closest flirtation with the 1,000-yard rushing barrier, missing out by 84 yards. He would carry the ball 185 times, averaging 5.0 a trip.

During the Golden Age, in a time that saw Ollie Matson running for the Cardinals, Frank Gifford for the Giants, Alan Ameche and Lenny Moore in Baltimore, McElhenny, remained the "King" of them all.

For a definitive view of his career, though, the record book runs a poor second to the artistry he brought to the game. The telling numbers took some digging.

For example, among backs who had rushed for more than 5,000 career yards during the 1950s, his 5,281 rushing yards ranked him as the fifth highest, while his 11,375 All-Purpose Yardage was fourth during the same era. He also ranked sixth for all-time in yards per carry with 4.70, and he still owns three of the four longest runs (89, 86, 82 yards) from scrimmage that's in the 49ers' record books.

"If I played with the guys today, I'd probably be just as good," said McElhenny. "They are bigger and faster, but I'd probably have been bigger and faster if I had the same training methods, the vitamins and all that."

11

Seattle Will Never Forget "The King"

The 49ers played numerous preseason games at the University of Washington stadium in Seattle. They made their first appearance in 1955 against the Giants, then again in 1957 and 1959 against the Cardinals. They also played the Cowboys in their inaugural NFL football game at that stadium in 1960.

McElhenny, a former Washington Huskie Hall of Famer and a 49er, left an indelible cleat mark on that stadium turf. More often than not, he played the role of the villain and helped knock over many hometown Husky and 49ers opponents.

Returning to Seattle where he set school records was always a heartwarming feeling for "The King." His sparkling runs were so numerous and they defy recounting. To name only a few which stand out is dangerous, but fans won't forget the 100-yard punt return down the sidelines against Southern California in 1951, nor the 77-yard gallop with a pass against Illinois, nor the 63-yard end sweep against Stanford that same season.

McElhenny's length-of-the-field run against the Trojans drew the last laugh. The Trojans were leading 13-7 at the time, and the game was nearing its conclusion. Des Koc, the Troy punter, booted the ball straight downfield towards the Washington end zone. McElhenny, in safety position, had his feet squarely planted on the goal line and everyone expected him to let the ball roll into the end zone for an automatic touchback.

A collective groan went up from the crowd as he elected to handle the punt, but it turned to a massive cheer when he sidestepped four would-be Trojan tacklers and broke into the clear at about his own 10-yard line. After that, it was just a matter of who could catch him, and nobody seriously entertained any thoughts that someone would.

All-American quarterback, Don Heinrich, a teammate of McElhenny in 1950-51 said: "Hugh had a sixth sense, with the kind of wide-angle vision that told him at a glance where every tackler was staked out. He had the complete repertoire of moves and an uncanny gift for breaking a tackle. He could do it all!"

McElhenny's long romp after taking a pass from Sam Mitchell in the Illinois game, likewise, brought the team from behind. Down two touchdowns, the Purple-clad Huskies were on the verge of being bounced completely out of contention.

McElhenny set out as a flanker and went straight downfield to take Mitchell's toss. He had to wait a couple of agonizing seconds for the ball, as it appeared a couple of Illinois defenders might get there in time to make the tackle. But as soon as the ball nestled in his arms, it was good-bye and six points. Fired up by the electrifying score, the Huskies bounced back to knot the count at 20-20 before losing in the final moments.

The same pattern was repeated against Stanford as McElhenny cut loose with a long 77-yard end sweep. Several Indians had a crack at him as he rounded the corner, but once he got to the sidelines with just a foot of running room, McElhenny was off to the races again.

From these three incidents—and many more like them—it's easy to see why McElhenny was the biggest name ever to play at the Stadium. His touchdowns—and they were many, of course—had a knack of showing up just when needed most.

"Accepting a handoff or taking a toss, McElhenny would break into the pursuit and accelerate in a way that appeared he was out-streaking his interference. More often than not, he would be cutting across the grain to pick up the block from a lineman or spread end who had just blipped into his periphery," said Cardinals' Woodley Lewis, describing McElhenny after a 27-21 loss to the 49ers in Seattle.

"The Stadium was one of the loudest stadiums I ever played in," said McElhenny. "I think the cantilevered metal roof trapped the sound, making it noisier. What made it unique was the fans came to our games by boat from Lake Washington. Often, they camped out all night in a boat just to get tickets. I always enjoyed playing there."

Other 49ers with ties to the Stadium:

Leo Nomellini: No single player typifies the villain more than Nomellini, a one-time Minnesota All-American linebacker. Who can forget the punishment he dealt to a rookie Husky quarterback, Anse McCulloch, in the 1948 opener at this stadium?

Washington was a great underdog and pinned its hopes on McCulloch's reputed right arm. Nomellini seldom let his arm get cranked. Booming through time after time, he dumped McCulloch unceremoniously, and even when his passes were completed, he seldom was on his feet to see the catch.

Doug Hogland: Oregon State's former guard still thought one of his greatest football thrills was the gloomy afternoon in 1951, when the Beavers came into the Stadium a ranked underdog and escaped with a remarkably easy 40-14 upset win. Hogland himself was a bearcat that day. OSC's fullback, Sam Baker, continuously moved up field on straight shots behind the blocking of Hogland. Nothing seemed to slow either man.

Matt Hazeltine: He teamed up for Cal's 27-6 win over Washington here in 1954. Paul Larson, an All-American quarterback pitched 11 strikes in 17 attempts. Meanwhile, Hazeltine, playing linebacker, was creating havoc with the Washington offense, helping keep Bobby Cox off balance. He even got a chance to carry the ball on a lateral off a pass interception—and made the most of it by galloping 20 yards before being brought down.

Bob Toneff: One of Notre Dame's finest tackles was just one of too many Irish for the Husky's team in 1949. His play in the line was superb, as Notre Dame crushed Washington, 27-7.

Bill Stits: An all-time UCLA great halfback never hit the headlines in a Seattle game, although he averaged 10 yards per carry and scored on a 46-yard pass reception in a 22-6 Bruins' win in 1954.

Fred Dugan: An ex-49er who played end for San Francisco (1958-59), had 7 receptions against the 49ers in Seattle, playing with the NFL expansion team, the Dallas Cowboys.

12

A Man for all Seasons

When one thinks of San Francisco greats of the Golden Age, names such as Perry, McElhenny, Tittle, and Nomellini will probably immediately come to mind. But no other 49ers' player made a deeper impression than Gordy LeRoy Soltau.

He was a tall Norwegian from Duluth, Minnesota. At six foot two, and 195 pounds, Soltau was a sure-handed receiver, a solid tackler and he could kick the daylights out of the ball. His achievements are unmistakable. As his stats show, Soltau was indeed the 49ers' man for all seasons.

"I won a California slalom championship and undoubtedly would've qualified as one of the nation's top skiers if I had been able to devote more time to the sport," said Soltau.

At the University of Minnesota, he was a top baseball pitcher and one of the few collegians who could play basketball and ice hockey during the same winter season. As one of the Gophers' ends, he won repeated All-Conference recognitions. He, along with Nomellini, played together on the 1949 Gopher team.

Soltau's college career was delayed by World War II as he enlisted in the Navy in 1942. After the war, Soltau was drafted by the Packers in the third round of the 1950 NFL draft. He didn't stay a Packer for long as he went to Cleveland, and then was sent to the 49ers for a fourth-round draft choice in 1951. The trade became known as one of the best trades the 49ers ever made.

"I was excited when I got traded to the 49ers," said Soltau, "when Coach Paul Brown told me, 'You can stay here, but the 49ers coach wants you so badly. I'm going to let you go if you want to go.'

"Brown said, 'You know you probably won't play much for us this year with Lou Groza as our kicker and Dante Lavelli and Max Speedie as our ends, but if you go to San Francisco, you can play right now.' So I said I'll go. I never regretted my decision to come to San Francisco.

"When I came to the 49ers, they were one heck of a team. Buck Shaw was the finest gentlemen I ever played football for. The thing that made him a great coach was his way of getting something extra out of his players who didn't know they had it. Teaming at first with Beals and then Wilson, I also became very familiar with quarterbacks Albert and Tittle," he said.

Soltau remembered Tittle as outstanding and as the possessor of a tremendous throwing arm, who took over the quarterbacking job full time in 1953 and went on to set a number of passing records. But he also had fond recollections of Albert, the little left-hander from Stanford.

"He was a great quarterback. He had great courage. He was a gamer. He loved to run the bootleg, and he was a wonderful punter. He was one of the only punters that could punt for the sidelines and be consistent with it. And he was a wonderful guy.

"My first year with the 49ers in 1950 we went 3-9, but we missed winning four or five games by a few points or a few inches. We never threw in the towel. That still rates as my favorite 49ers' team I played on.

"I played four positions in my first season with the 49ers. I saw the most action primarily at defensive end, on the kickoff units and at offensive end. When kicker Joe "The Toe" Ventrano was released in training camp, I became the man for PATs and field goals."

As a receiver and kicker, Soltau led the 49ers in scoring with 44 points his first season. He was a game saver, a clutch guy. In 1951, during a 44-17 win over the Rams, he was installed as a receiver and scored 26 points on three touchdown receptions, a field goal, and five extra points. In 1952 he caught 10 passes for 190 yards against the Giants.

"My biggest thrills were beating the Rams twice in 1953, once in Los Angeles where I caught the last minute pass and we won 31-27, and the other at Kezar.

"The Rams were ahead 20-0 in the second quarter and we wound up winning it 31-30, and I kicked the winning field goal with five seconds left. Detroit won the division, but still teams feared us. You whispered McElhenny or Brown and our opponents began to shiver. In 1956, I kicked four field goals to beat the Rams 33-30.

"We finished 9-3 that year, and we were in the race until the final day," said Soltau.

Soltau had first seen McElhenny in college when he kicked off to him when Minnesota played Washington in 1949. He proceeded to do with that kickoff what he would do so many times over the next 15 years—break off an electrifying touchdown run of 100 yards, in which he ran every which way, eluding tacklers, some of whom Soltau recalled had more than one shot at him.

When Soltau came on the scene, players could still get up and run with the ball after they were down. They changed the rule, because at times they'd have nine guys on top of a ball carrier or receiver. Then they'd blow the whistle after their forward motion was stopped.

"You can't imagine how many cheap shots we took," Soltau said. "Sometimes it was like we'd have to stop breathing before they'd blow a whistle. You don't see blockers and tacklers using their shoulders the way we used to. Instead, they snap their necks and lead with their helmets."

So who was the toughest teammate on the team during his career?

"No doubt, Hardy Brown," said Soltau. "He would literally throw himself into the wedge or a defender and knock him out. Ball carriers hated the thought of coming into contact with him.

"I remember one game against Detroit in 1953 when Brown was blindsided by "Wild Horse" Mains, who tore open Brown's thigh. I mean tore it wide open. So they took him in the dressing room and put 37 stitches in his leg, and there he was back on the field again playing the whole second half. He was tough as nails."

Soltau rated linebacker Don Paul of the Rams, along with George Connor of the Bears, as the two best of the toughest defensive players he ever played against, as well as Yale Lary, Jim David of Detroit, and "Night Train" Lane of the Rams also as great defenders.

"They all knew how to hold me up. Today they call it 'bump and run.' I used to lie awake nights thinking of playing against these guys," said Soltau.

"My last year was in 1958; it was a pretty trying year for me. At the time I was 34, and Albert announced his retirement, and I was reduced to just placekicking. Our new coach, Red Hickey, invited me to camp in 1959, on what amounted to a 'tryout,' but I felt that would've made it embarrassing whether I made the club or not, so I retired instead with all my body parts intact."

Off the field, Soltau was a pioneer in advancing benefits for NFL football players. He was the first player representative for the 49ers when the Players Association was formed in 1954, and for his work as the team players' rep, he earned the nickname "The Senator."

Soltau retired in 1958, scoring 644 points (25 touchdowns, 70 field goals and 284 Pats), and led the team in scoring in eight of his nine seasons, and is the fifth-leading scorer in 49ers history. He was All-Pro in 1952, 1953 and 1954, and he was selected to the 1951, 1952 and 1953 Pro Bowls.

13

Hardy "Hatchet" Brown

Oh, what shoulders he had! There has never been anyone like Hardy Brown and there never will be. Who could forget Brown? As legend has it, as a linebacker he knocked out more than 20 opponents during the 49ers' 1951 season. He was the epitome of the NFL's active wild-and-crazy hitters.

After seeing action in the Pacific as a Marine paratrooper during World War II, and then spending three seasons terrorizing the Missouri Valley Conference as a blocking back and linebacker at Tulsa University, Brown had a long and productive career as a pro.

He learned the shoulder tackle (he rarely used his arms) when he played at Tulsa. But, he only perfected the maneuver there. He learned it from his older brother, Jeff, when they were growing up at a Fort Worth orphanage. However, football never quite dispelled the fury that burned behind the blue eyes of Brown.

Hardy left a trail of broken body parts all over the place during his five seasons he was with the 49ers (1951-55). He was only six feet tall and weighed 195 pounds, and he wasn't very fast or tall. But in his case, it meant practically nothing. The only thing that mattered was that devastating right shoulder, which he used the way a boxer delivers a six-inch knockout punch—something in a way Heavyweight Champion Joe Louis did. But the years didn't mellow him much.

Dewitt "Tex" Coulter, an All-Pro tackle with the Giants said: "The first time I played against him as a pro, I came out of the huddle at the beginning of the game and I figured I'd say hello. I came up to the line and looked across at his linebacker spot, and his eyes looked like they belonged to some cave animal. They were fiery and unfocused. You didn't know if he could see anything or everything. I kept my mouth shut."

Later, at a Los Angeles hotel before a Pro Bowl game, Coulter ran into Brown and Jim Finks, who had been a teammate of Brown's at Tulsa. "Old Hardy liked to drink a little and have a good time," Coulter recalled, "but he was real silent that day. He finally said, 'You know, I hate everybody in this whole goddamned world.' I said, 'Do you hate me?' Brown thought a while and said, 'No, not you.'"

"Pound for pound, inch for inch," said Tittle, "he was the toughest football player I ever met. He was so tough he was damned near illegal. I played with him for five years and saw him do things that were almost unbelievable. While playing the Redskins, I watched him knock out the entire starting backfield, leaving only Harry Gilmer, their quarterback, in one piece. When I say 'knocked out,' I mean that literally!"

NFL halfbacks particularly had vivid memories of him. They would tell you, usually with a wince of pain that had never quite gone away, what it was like to be hit by Brown's sledgehammer shoulder.

"I didn't really believe the things I'd heard about him, but then I played against him for the first time at Kezar in 1951," said Joe Geri, a single-wing tailback for the Steelers.

"We ran a trap or something, and he threw that shoulder into my eye—we didn't wear face masks in those days—and put me down on my back. I was lying there groggy, but I managed to ask one of my teammates, 'Is this bad?' And he said, 'Well, your eye's out.'"

It was reported that Geri's eye literally was hanging by a tendon out of the socket. "I walked to the sidelines and one of my teammates said, 'Don't worry Joe, we'll take care of Brown.'"

But when it was all over, he'd put about three more players, besides Geri, out of the game. In all fairness, Brown was an ideal middle linebacker in the 49ers' 5-3 defense, because his duties were easy. His main job was plugging holes when the guard pulled. Most of his tackles were made in the middle of the line at point-blank range.

"It was all technique and timing," said St. Clair. "He would coil like a snake and then explode in mid-air! He'd extend the shoulder and aim it at your Adam's apple. You either got hit in the chest or the face. He destroyed people with it."

"Guys would be cornered and try to run Hardy over," said Rex Berry, "but he'd just get lower and then pop! He'd snap up under a guy's jaw. He ended a lot of careers. I always thought, boy, I'm glad he's on my team."

Brown was such a force that some people around the league figured he must have been doing something outside the rules.

"They thought maybe he was using a steel plate or something," said Buck Shaw. "Halas, the Bears' coach, sent an official into our locker room right after one game. They made Hardy take off his shoulder pads, thinking he had some metal in there. Nothing was found."

Hardy occasionally could be a brawler off the field, as well as on, but his 49er teammates recall him as a quiet guy they got along with just fine.

"He kept to himself a lot," said Soltau, "but he was a nice kid, a good teammate."

The 49ers might not have felt that way if Brown had used that vicious shoulder against them in practice, but he didn't get the chance.

The coaching staff wouldn't let him play in scrimmages. When the game started, it was a different matter.

Offering confirmation, GM Lou Spadia remembered one exhibition game in Omaha against the Cardinals: "In those days, you played where you could, and we played on a baseball field where they refused to remove the mound. Hardy caught Elmer Angsman coming down off the mound while he was coming up, and he gave him an unbelievable hit. It was like running into a wall. He knocked the guy out."

The 49ers used to watch Brown on game films and marvel. "We'd cheer and laugh," said St. Clair. "A guy 260 pounds would be running down the field, and we'd see Hardy stalking him. Then bang! He'd turn the guy upside down."

Linebacker Chuck Bednarik of the Eagles always said Brown was the dirtiest SOB he ever played against. Hardy always played tough, but he seemed to be at his best when the 49ers were playing their rivals, the Rams. Glenn "Mr. Outside" Davis, the Rams' talented halfback, had his career, in effect, ended by Brown in a game in which his famed shoulder tackle hit him so hard that ligaments were torn in both of Glenn's knees.

Davis was never the same again and quit football shortly thereafter. Another Rams' running back, Dick Hoerner, was knocked out cold for 15 minutes after meeting Brown head-on at the line of scrimmage.

"I don't hold out any real venom for him," said Davis, "but I think he made a mistake playing the way he did. He would have been a much better player if he had concentrated on making the tackle instead of trying to kill somebody."

"But even though he would try to knock the hell out of you with that shoulder, I don't think it was a dirty blow. I was a teammate of his for a while at Washington, and I thought the world of him personally," said halfback Bill Dudley of the Redskins.

Shaw frequently got on Brown for missing tackles while he was trying to deliver the shoulder blow. "But if he hadn't been able to hit like that, he never would have played football," commented Shaw.

Brown's tactics often made opponents attempt to retaliate, nearly always without success. "Some teams would put a little money pool to see who could get Hardy out of the game," said St. Clair. "You'd watch on films, and they'd all be going after him on some plays. But he was cunning and crafty. He almost never took any solid hits."

Even when he did, it didn't seem to matter much. In 1954, in a game against Detroit, Brown shattered the nose of halfback, "Bullet" Bill Bowman with a shoulder tackle. "I couldn't believe Brown did that. I always admired him," said Bowman.

"Think of it this way," said Tittle. "What he was all about in football wasn't just physical; he was a psychic occurrence, hammering everything and everyone in sight. One day I said to him, 'Hardy, I think you'd pop that shoulder into your own mother.' He replied with, 'Not unless she had a football under her arm, Y. A.'"

Teams always were very much aware of Brown's presence when they played the 49ers. "When they came up to the line of scrimmage, the first thing they'd do was find out where Hardy was," St. Clair said. "The battle cry of the league was, 'Where's Hardy?'"

His style was not without cost. He was one of the first players to wear a face mask, which probably saved his profile at least.

"He always had a sore shoulder," said Soltau. "Nobody could have played in the beaten-up condition he was in, but he played anyway. In his last year with the team, his arthritis in that right shoulder made it tough for Brown to lift his arm or even to scratch his head."

Brown will always be remembered as a once-in-a-lifetime player. He is one of only two players (the other, Ben Agajanian of the Giants) to ever have played in the AAFC, the NFL and the AFL. He was the most unique player ever.

14

Mr. Versatility

To many, Charley Powell is considered one of the most highly rated multi-talented athletes of his generation. There were many great two-sport athletes who played professional football, like Jim Thorpe, Ollie Matson, Deion Sanders and Bo Jackson, but none made the impact of Powell, one of the youngest athletes ever to play in the NFL.

That means a lot when you consider the amazing talent that has graced the 49ers' organization since the team's beginning in 1946. And the 49ers had some Olympic track stars like Renaldo Nehemiah and Bob Hayes. Jimmy Johnson was also an amazing athlete and a brother to Olympic Decathlon champion, Rafer Johnson.

In high school in San Diego, the six foot three, 230 pound Powell, was a 12-time letterman in football, basketball, baseball and track. As a baseball player, he hit home runs out of Balboa Stadium that reportedly made Hall of Famer Ted Williams envious.

He was California State Football "Prep Player of the Year" in back-to-back seasons, 1950 and 1951, and he was named to the All-America High School team. While participating in track, Powell ran the 100 yards in 9.6 seconds, high jumped six feet two inches and threw the shotput 57 feet 9 ¼ inches—which to this day remains the standard for a high school in San Diego.

He was such an outstanding basketball player that when the Harlem Globetrotters came to town, they tried to persuade his parents to allow them to sign him to a contact and take him on the road with them. They refused, and Powell remained in high school.

As a senior, he used to stop along the way to school at the home of World Light Heavyweight Champion, Archie Moore. Each morning, he and Archie would spar: a high school kid and the Champion of the World. Powell would hold his own against the Champ. In addition, he brought in money to help his family while boxing at military bases.

After being recruited by Notre Dame and UCLA to play football, Powell instead decided on playing professional baseball. While still in high school, owner Bill Veeck, who owned the American League St. Louis Browns, signed the power-hitting right fielder to a contract in 1952.

Powell spent the summer playing Class B ball in Stockton and then in Idaho before forsaking baseball to play in the NFL. Remarkably, Powell accomplished this during a time that saw Jackie Robinson breaking the color barrier in professional baseball.

At the urging of 49ers' quarterback Frankie Albert, he and Buck Shaw drove to San Diego. It was there they met up with his parents, where they signed Powell as a 19-year-old free agent to a contract that required his parents' signature.

Powell was one of the few players who made it in the NFL without playing college football. In his first season as a 49er in 1952, he earned $10,000.

On October 12, he made a stunning 49ers debut as a starting defensive end, playing alongside Nomellini against the Lions. His performance was possibly the greatest single game feat in 49er history.

Phil Bengston, the team's defensive line coach, instructed Powell to rush Detroits' All-Pro quarterback, Bobby Layne, as hard as he could.

It certainly paid off as Powell spent the afternoon making life miserable for Layne and his All-Pro offensive line by sacking him 10 times (this was before sacks were officially counted in the NFL), for a minus 67 yards. Layne failed to complete a pass until the fourth quarter, as the 49ers crushed the Lions, 28-0.

49ers' tackle Bob Toneff said of Powell: "He went berserk. He was a terror today! His performance was so inspirational that we awarded him the game ball."

Powell played five seasons (55 games) for the 49ers (1952-53 and 55-57). Between stints with the 49ers, he also had visions of becoming a World's Heavyweight Boxing Champion.

He boxed professionally, beginning in 1954. He took the entire year off from the gridiron to pursue his boxing career. RING magazine declared him the best boxer ever to come out of another pro sport, and he was rated among the best young heavyweights in the country.

But after suffering three broken hands, he decided to return his energies to football and returned to the 49ers in 1955.

After his NFL career, Powell would continue on as a fighter. On March 4, 1959, he knocked out second-ranked heavyweight challenger Nino Valdez in Miami. He rose as high as No. 4 in the RING magazine heavyweight rankings, finishing with 25 wins, 11 loses, 3 draws and 17 knockouts.

Upon his retirement from boxing, Powell said: "The human head was not meant to be punched. But when you talk about hurting all over, in football a lot of times three or four months after you play, you'd reach out to pick up a glass of water and you'd feel it in your shoulders, back and arms."

Powell was a world-class athlete long before players were fairly compensated for their skills. He credited his success as a football player (and later a boxer) to his superior conditioning. There have been other NFL players who tried and failed to duplicate what Powell had done.

Sports Illustrated columnist Jim Murray wrote: "Powell compared favorably to the greatest all-around athletes in American history, noting that Jim Thorpe and Jackie Robinson never had to tee it up with Heavyweight Champions of the World. There was nothing in sports that Charlie Powell couldn't do."

15

Mr. Meaner

John Henry Johnson, a six-foot-two, 225-pound running back was nicknamed "Mr. Meaner" because of his viciousness as a ball carrier. He often was compared to his counterpart, the elusive Hugh McElhenny, as that of a wild boar on the hoof for battle.

His roughhouse running style was punishing to all who got in his way, regardless if ran inside or outside. His manner, if he was on the field into today's era of players, would be considered that of being a multi-tasker, as his style of play enabled him to block. Then while playing on the other side of the ball, he could cover and play with the best of them.

"I was durable and tough, some say dirty, giving always to retaliation," said Johnson. "I played halfback on offense and safety and linebacker on goal line defense."

Johnson was a high school football and basketball star and ran track in Pittsburgh, California, before going on to play football at St. Mary's College. While there, he held the distinction of being the first black athlete ever to compete against the University of Georgia in football.

After St. Mary's dropped the sport, he turned his attention to the University of San Francisco, with the hope of continuing his football career, but the admission department refused to admit him.

The Dons football team would complete the 1951 season unbeaten and untied before the school administrators dropped the sport all together.

"Blocking for John Henry in the same backfield with Matson and Toler would have been a dream come true, but it just didn't happen," said St. Clair.

Johnson would eventually join several former St. Mary's teammates at Arizona State. It was there he earned All-Border Conference honors.

His talents caught the eye of the NFL's Steelers who drafted him in the second round of the 1953 NFL draft. But Johnson signed instead with the Calgary Stampeders in the Canadian Football League (at a higher salary), playing with former 49ers' quarterback, Frankie Albert.

Johnson would eventually be awarded the CFL's Most Valuable Player Award. Albert called him "one of the toughest running backs he'd ever seen."

While under contract with Calgary, the Steelers traded his rights to the 49ers, and Johnson returned to the States to play, beginning with the 1954 season.

The 49ers secretly signed him while he was still in the CFL, a deal that enraged league officials. Once in San Francisco, he would join the other three future Hall of Famers (Tittle, Perry and McElhenny) in the same backfield, dubbed "The Million Dollar Backfield."

"He was as fast as Perry and Mac," Tittle said, "but people didn't think of him that way. He had the hands for catching passes, and he would have caught more, if he had not been so valuable as a blocker in the backfield. He was a perfect complement to McElhenny's elusive moves and Perry's inside power."

His role in his rookie season was that as a primary blocker, but he would produce some outstanding numbers in the 12 games he played in. He would rush for 681 yards and 9 touchdowns, while hauling in 28 passes, and he would earn a spot on the 1954 Pro Bowl Roster.

Johnson's demeanor resembled back-alley brawls, as the league came to fear No. 35 because of his crushing blocks and tackles, which led to a couple of players ending up with a broken jaw; one was his own teammate during an intra-squad scrimmage.

"What did you want me to do?" an unapologetic Johnson asked. "Kiss the guy or tackle him?"

"He was mean," St. Clair said. "He could have been heavyweight champion, if he were a fighter. Football was like a combat zone for him. He carried the impact to the opponent. If he'd waited for contact, the impact would have been on him. He was one of the few runners who would look for somebody to hit.

"He'd go out of his way to hurt people, and if I didn't get out of his way, he'd run right up my back like a tractor! But every once in a while, instead of trying to dodge his opponent, he would run around them. What he brought to the game was strength, malice and an unrelenting running style. He would attack a brick wall!"

In a 1955 exhibition game, Johnson smashed into Cardinals' star Charley Trippi so hard, he sustained multiple face fractures. That blow and his other hard hits, which would have gained him a reputation around the league as a dirty player, could have delayed his enshrinement in the Hall of Fame. But Johnson always maintained that he had only a "do unto others" philosophy, noting his own lasting football injuries.

Despite the dangers of his sport, Johnson wore just a single-bar face mask on his helmet and no pads or gloves on his hands. His stiff arm, essentially an open-palm punch to the jaw while running at full speed, was devastating.

"If you didn't keep your eye on him," linebacker Wayne Walker, with the Lions, told the *San Francisco Chronicle*, "the next thing you know you'd have your jaw wired."

(Author's note: My Dad told me that I would always be able to single out Johnson from the rest of the halfbacks by the style of leather helmet he wore. It was made by Wilson.)

Like many of the big backs during the 1950s, Johnson's value exceeded the number of yards he gained. He was an intimidator, whether he had the ball or not.

"You've got to scare your opponent," he said. "I could run away from a lot of guys after I got them afraid of a collision with me. I always dished out more than I can take."

Over a three-year span, beginning in 1954, Johnson's career would take on as many changes. For example, a shoulder injury limited his play in 1955, then a year later a change in the team's offensive formation, which resulted in him playing less. Then just before the start of the 1957 season, he was traded to the Lions and promptly helped the team win an NFL championship.

16

The Rifleman

The phrase, "The Golden Age of Pro Football" is somewhat inaccurate. It should have been called, "The Golden Age of Offense." Especially gilded in the 1950s were quarterbacks with big arms, gutty leaders, field generals, who took charge in the huddle. They called their own games and, generally speaking, drove a team to victory or loss with the strength of their arms.

Y. A. Tittle was one of them. It's been said he was one of the greatest quarterbacks to ever play the game. The 49ers' signal caller would go by many names, even so far as to explain what the Y. and A. stood for in his name. He stated that the Y. was for Yelberton, while the A. was short for Abraham.

In addition, fans choose to call him "Yat," or in reference to his thinning hairline, Y. A. was often referred to as "The Bald Eagle" and "Colonel Slick," as well as to his manner of firing his forward passes.

Whatever nickname he was known by, Tittle had a cannon for an arm. He threw sidearm, thus giving the ball a unique trajectory with a lot of velocity.

Football was Tittle's life since his high school days in Marshall, Texas. He spent four years at LSU and was All-American after his senior season. He capped off his career in the Louisiana bayou by being named MVP of the 1947 Cotton Bowl Classic, which ended in a scoreless tie between LSU and Arkansas, as the teams battled through a wild ice storm.

He is remembered best as being drafted in the first round in 1948 by Detroit, with the sixth overall selection in the annual NFL draft. However, Tittle shunned the Lions and signed with the AAFC Browns for a $10,000 salary, with a bonus of $2,000.

At the time, the AAFC Colts were in dire straits and facing bankruptcy. The city's business leaders formed a "Save the Colts Committee" to raise money, but the team was in need of more player personnel.

With Coach Paul Brown of the Browns and owner Ben Lindheimer of the Rams as directors, they would submit a list of potential AAFC players from the rosters of the leagues' teams aimed at helping the fledgling Colts' roster.

Tittle was added to the list, and the Browns in turn sent the quarterback to the Colts. Tittle would play two seasons with Baltimore (one of the three teams—along with San Francisco and Cleveland—that were incorporated into the NFL) following the folding of the AAFC.

Tittle's passing philosophy was established as a rookie by Colts' head coach Cecil Isbell, who had thrown all those passes to Don Hutson at Green Bay.

"Depend on yourself to complete the pass," Isbell told Tittle. "Throw the damned ball! The only one you can count on for help is your receiver. Don't wait for a pass pattern to spring a guy open so you can lay it in his lap. Your mother-in-law can do that."

When the Colts folded after the 1950 season, all of their players were mixed in with the college draft of 1951, where the 49ers made their future quarterback the third overall selection.

"I remember they threw me in a pool with other players and we were re-drafted," said Tittle. "After I got the news, I was happy to come to San Francisco. To me it was a great honor because they had such a good tradition."

Tittle came to the 49ers with three years pro experience and found himself initially in the unfamiliar position of backup to quarterback Albert. But Tittle was known for his pocket presence. He was a fighter and did not take crap from anybody.

"Albert was more of a roll-out quarterback," said Tittle. "He used a lot of play action and was unpredictable. I was more of a drop-back passer, so defenses had to shift according to our styles. The bootleg is another thing I learned from Albert. He was a great field general, a great leader."

In training camp, the newly drafted Tittle approached Albert and asked about some minor point for a play. Albert made a face and said, "Hey, Tittle, you know you're after my job."

But late in the season, Tittle began to make his move. He came on in relief and pulled out a couple of big wins. Buck Shaw had a thriving offense and a mediocre defense.

"Buck never cared much about defense," said Albert. "He drafted for offense, and all the guys who couldn't run, he put on defense."

Shaw did as much for Tittle's psychological approach to the game as Isbell did for his confidence in his passing game. He treated Tittle like a man and as a pro. There was nothing Tittle wanted more to do than to win for him.

The game had changed a little bit for Tittle. There was definitely still a T-formation and a need for clever ball-handling skills as quarterback. So Albert was really more of a total quarterback and sophisticated at bootlegging. Once Tittle went into a game, it changed to an almost entire passing game.

"It changed in my favor in a way because the game had changed to a quarterback with passing," declared Tittle. "That's all I really did. Ball handling didn't mean too much anymore, which was good for me. I called my own plays and rarely audibled.

"The game was so different in the 1950s, as we did not study two sets of films before each game. We did not think about the pass rushers, we never studied automatics, we didn't even have automatics! There was none of the preparation we know today. In those days, the average lifespan of a pro was three to four years."

In 1952, Shaw attempted a rotation system similar to what the Rams were doing with Waterfield and Van Brocklin. Albert would start and play the first and third quarters of a game, Tittle the second and the fourth. The next week they would alternate.

The system worked for a while, but it was really an appeasement for the players and fans, doomed as much as anything from the law of averages.

Tittle said, "Too many times, the guy with the hot hand was sitting on the bench, while the cold guy was in. Because pass rushers were ferocious and blocking often minimal, I had to throw in a hurry, which meant frequent throwaways. A 50 percent completion and 260 yards passing was a good game in those days."

Albert retired from the 49ers in 1953 but found his way to the Canadian Football League. Tittle became the starting quarterback, making his mark both as a field general and passer.

He became the ringmaster in the 49ers' explosive offense. He had a strong arm, as he could rifle the football 25, 30, 40 yards on a line to his receivers: Wilson, Soltau, Conner or Owens.

"I could always throw, and I was confident of my calls, as I understood the game and I would play hurt. Shaw never second-guessed my decisions," said Tittle.

In his first full season in 1953 as the 49ers' starting quarterback, he tied Albert's club record of five touchdown passes in one game, while setting a single-game franchise record with 29 completions and 371 passing yards, in a 45-14 drubbing of the Colts at Kezar.

He finished the season with 20 touchdown passes, leading the team to a 9-3-0 mark. His outstanding play would also earn him a trip to the Pro Bowl.

Enthusiasm was a key to the Texas-born Tittle way of playing through numerous injuries, such as a shattered cheekbone, a broken hand or toe.

He also could claim what no 49er ever had—or will ever have, as he became the first to grace the cover of Sports Illustrated that debuted in 1954. That was the same year the 49ers' backfield was dubbed "The Million Dollar Backfield" by publicist Dan McGuire as among the best of all-time.

The quartet of Tittle, McElhenny, Johnson and Perry played together in the "Wonder Bread era" from 1954-56, but they played only for working man's pay. In fact, a million dollars in those days might have been the entire player salary budget for several seasons. (McGuire must have counted on inflation when he gave the foursome the name).

"A very figurative label," said GM Spadia. "Their salaries probably didn't even add up to $100,000, but they were unparalleled, as far as talent was concerned."

"I couldn't have asked for two better backs than McElhenny and Perry. They could run both inside and outside, catch the ball and block," said Tittle. "They made me look good for many years we played together. Johnson played here for a couple of years and was a force to deal with. If you got in his way, he bruised you up. He was like a cannonball."

Over a three-year period, the foursome arguably had one of pro football's greatest offensive backfields.

"We were always called heroes but never champions," said Tittle regretfully.

After three non-winning seasons, the 1957 season proved to be a landmark year for Tittle, as he would play in his first postseason game and earn his third trip to the Pro Bowl. He would finish in the top three in several key stats.

His 2,157 passing yards were good for second best of all NFL quarterbacks, and he threw 13 touchdown passes and a career-high 63.1 in pass completions (a mark he would never surpass during the rest of his time in the league), finishing second and first, respectively. He was named UPI's NFL player of the year.

Ironically, Tittle is remembered best for a gimmick, the "alley-oop" play, where he would team up with the six-foot-three acrobatic receiver, R. C. Owens, on a pass play born by accident that became a calculated pass play.

Tittle would loft a high, usually wobbly, 35- to 45-yard pass, and Owens would out-leap his defenders, just as he did as a hoopster in college.

But for Tittle, the 1957 season was one of triumph and agony. Last-second victories became a 49ers' trademark. "We won five games in the last couple of minutes," said Tittle.

Though, the 49ers' chance at a championship berth came to an abrupt end, as Detroit claimed the Western Division playoff contest against the 49ers.

That defeat to the Lions would indelibly live on as the signature game of the 49ers throughout the decade. It is a pity Tittle never put the arm on a championship team as a 49er, or any of the other teams that he would play for over the next seven years. A championship was his "white whale." He always committed his body and soul to its capture. Sometimes winning isn't everything; it is the will to win and that is the only thing...and that would carry Tittle to being enshrined into the Pro Football Hall of Fame.

Looking back, Tittle did pretty darn well. He had a career that lasted 16 years. In three seasons with the Baltimore Colts and 10 as a 49er, before he was shuffled off to the New York Giants, he would throw for roughly 14 miles, thus earning him the title of "The Rifleman."

17

The Fighting Spirit

Joe Arenas was just 19 years of age when he and his fellow Marines were part of the second wave that climbed the sandy banks of Iwo Jima, recorded as the bloodiest Pacific battle of World War II. It was 36 days of intense shelling and bombing, commencing in February 1945.

"I was just 138 pounds, but I felt so much bigger serving my country. I was a Marine," Arenas said. "That's where I wanted to be. That's the uniform I wanted."

Just days into battle, Arenas was digging a foxhole trying to make it just a little deeper and safer, when an incredible pain struck his back. He had been shot as the shrapnel missed his spinal cord by a fraction of an inch.

"All of a sudden, it was like an ax hit me in the back, hotter than heck," he said. "My buddy who was in the foxhole with me said, 'Man, I got to get you out of here.'"

His corporal dragged Arenas down to the beach. As he laid upon a stretcher surrounded by bodies, he himself could barely move. Thus Arenas was unable to escape the sulfurous fumes that was all around the black lunar soil on the beach.

Medical personnel scrambled to attend to everybody. Then, after what seemed an eternity to those on that historic beach amid gunfire explosions, Arenas was among those fortunate enough to eventually find safety.

"We were supposed to go into that island and just walk through it," he expressed. "We bombarded that island for three or four months, or better. I don't know why it didn't sink. We didn't expect any Japanese out there, but here they were, all over the place. How they survived, how they lived there, I don't know."

Granted a medical discharge, Arenas spent time in Navy hospitals in Salem, Oregon and San Diego before making his way back to his home in Nebraska.

After enrolling at the University of Nebraska, recurring back trouble forced him to miss class work, and with his eligibility in jeopardy, he transferred to Omaha University for the 1948-49 school year, which had just reinstated sports following the war. He was in less pain now, as he intended only to run track and play basketball. However, coaches convinced him to give football a try.

"I didn't even know how to put on my shoulder pads when I first suited up for tryouts," said Arenas. "Once everything was where it was supposed to be, it all came naturally to me."

Arenas played halfback in a single-wing, affording him the opportunity to both run and pass. It was a combination he parlayed into 1,612 total yards in just eight games as a 1949 All-American.

"In those days, we called our own plays. I wasn't a big man at five foot eleven, but I had a good mind and I made plays," said Arenas. "In one game, I was playing on a sore knee, and I threw for 219 yards and four touchdowns (a school record then), in a 38-26 loss to Wayne State that closed out the 1949 season."

It didn't end there. The 49ers picked Arenas in the eighth round of the 1951 draft. "Playing with the 49ers gave me the attitude that 'You can't hurt me,'" stated Arenas.

He immediately leaped into action again, playing halfback and adding value to his game by returning kickoffs and punts.

"Playing in a backfield with Albert, Tittle, Perry and the spectacular McElhenny, we captured everything but an NFL championship," claimed Arenas.

Arenas was recognized by his own team and opponents as one of the most perilous members. Tittle recalls how Arenas had that "fighting spirit" when his number was called.

"He was a spark plug and infected the rest of the team. He was our teams' "holler guy," with his continuous enthusiastic stream of character and exhortation," declared Tittle.

The way Arenas saw it, sprinting through a pack of snorting football players was a heck of a lot easier than his previous occupation as a U.S. Marine.

"I remember looking down the line and thinking, what was there to be scared of? I'm as good as any of these people," he said.

"Often, because of our shaky defense, I was called upon to play defensive back, and virtually I saw 60 minutes of action. The roughness and toughness I possessed was attributed to the training I received in the Marines."

Arenas went on to become the 49ers' top punt and kickoff return man. But kickoff duty was a walk in the park for him as compared to the day he was hit by shrapnel.

When he hauled in a punt or a kickoff, 49ers' fans were ready for fireworks. He could streak down the field at full speed and turn on a dime, leaving tacklers falling over themselves trying to catch him.

He led the NFL in kickoff returns in 1953, averaging a healthy 34.4 yards, which has remained the 49ers' single season standard.

On December 16, 1955, Arenas was on his way to a 94-yard kickoff return for a touchdown against the Colts at Kezar, but he failed to reach the end zone.

Arenas jokingly told reporters after the game, "My elastic on this stocking snapped, and I thought my pants were falling off, so I slowed down short of the goal line."

In 1957, Arenas old back problems had flared up again, and he ended his NFL career at the end of the season. He played in 84 games over seven seasons, rushing for 987 yards and catching passes for 675 more, with a total of 16 touchdowns.

He also returned 124 punts for 774 yards and 139 kickoffs for 3,798 yards, as each would net him another touchdown. He also realized that none of this could have happened after being in a shallow grave, as many others did, during the bloody battle at Iwo Jima.

18

The "Geek"

Bob St. Clair was the tallest player in the NFL at six foot nine, and a lean 263 pounds of muscle. Fittingly, he spent his entire pro career playing with the 49ers. The native San Franciscan played all his games on the turf of Kezar Stadium: two years when he was at Polytechnic High School, three at the University of San Francisco, and 12 years as a star tackle with the 49ers.

He admitted, "I was never in a losing football game in high school or college, and I just played tackle year after year. It was a way of life. I'd pull out and lead plays around the end, and I was pretty fast. I could do the 100 in 11 flat."

St. Clair had size, speed, intelligence and a love for hitting. But it would be his "flamboyant" lifestyle that made many stand up and notice. He spent the early part of his career wearing a leather helmet without a face mask, because he believed that big men didn't wear masks.

Because of this stance, he broke his nose six times, played an entire quarter with a broken shoulder, and once stayed in a game after a blocked kick, resulting in the loss of five teeth. He was one of the best run-and-pass blockers in the league. And he protected his quarterbacks, including his first-year roommate, Tittle, and later Brodie.

"Our 1951 Dons team was considered one of the greatest college teams of all time. Ten of their starters became NFL draft picks, with three, Ollie Matson, Gino Marchetti, and myself, have been inducted into the Pro Football Hall of Fame.

"We were unbeaten and hoping for an Orange Bowl bid. However, the Orange Bowl organizers had one condition. If invited, we would have to leave our two African American players, Matson and Burl Toler, at home. We told them to go to hell!" he said.

Following the 1951 season, the Dons dropped their football program and St. Clair transferred to the University of Tulsa for his senior year. His heart, however, remained in San Francisco.

Tulsa finished the year at 8-1-1 and received an invitation to the Gator Bowl. His outstanding play would earn St. Clair an opportunity to live out his boyhood dream—to play in the East-West All-Star Game at Kezar.

St. Clair was drafted by the 49ers in the third round in 1953, as he held firm in salary talks. "They offered me only $5,500 and I insisted on $6,000," he stated. "I had to hold out a whole week and eventually got my way, because the 49ers were desperate for an offensive tackle. It was a pittance compared to the millions that top college players earn today."

He would make an immediate impact in training camp with his strength and toughness. For example, when he would hit the two-man sled so hard, he not only didn't just move it back, he literally knocked it over.

In addition, when he hit the mammoth, dangling tackling dummy called, "Big Bertha," the dummy split in half, sawdust and all into bits and pieces. St. Clair showed his toughness before he knew his playbook.

He was given the nickname "The Geek" by his teammate Bruno Banducci because of his unusual habits of eating uncooked meat. He came up with the name after watching an old-time movie, where Tyrone Power would eat live chickens in a carnival sideshow.

St. Clair's would eat raw liver, dove and quail, including their hearts. He liked everything raw and preferably cold. His affinity for eating raw meat frightened his teammates, as he would admit that it brought out the "animal" instinct in him.

"There was already bad blood between the 49ers and the Eagles team," he noted. "In a preseason game with the Eagles in Texas, a riot broke out when 49ers' defensive end, Charlie Powell, started a fight. And when the Eagles showed up for our home opener at Kezar, all hell broke loose.

"McElhenny started chasing the Eagles' Pete Pihos with his helmet and eventually catching him and whacking him over the head. Both benches cleared. Everybody was fighting in the end zone. I got a few good licks in myself. Fans were throwing bottles and cans. Joe McTigue, the 49er band leader, was trying to play "The Star-Spangled Banner" to maybe restore some order, but the guys were being thrown into the bandstand, knocking the instruments off their stands."

Against the Browns in Cleveland, St. Clair and the Browns' Don Joyce got into a melee. "We were really going at it. Punches were flying on the first play from scrimmage. First Joyce punched me, then I punched Joyce," he said.

It didn't take the 49ers long to realize St. Clair was out to beat his competition, one way or another. During his first three seasons with the 49ers, he played offensive tackle and defensive tackle and would play mostly on the offensive side for the latter part of his 11-year career.

He would block for Tittle, and running backs Perry, McElhenny and Johnson—as each have earned a spot in the Pro Football Hall of Fame. It's no secret that the 49ers talented backfield made a lot of impressive plays in the 1950s, and St. Clair did in fact had much to do with it.

"I made them famous," he said. "It was always a challenge. I tried to do the best I could. Luckily, most of the time it was good enough for Tittle to throw the ball or allow big runs by my guys. I knew if I made my block pulling around the end and took out the linebacker coming up, or the defensive back, that one of the guys behind me was going to make a lot of yardage."

Like everybody else, St. Clair found himself checking out the impressive running styles of the 49ers' talented running backs.

"I especially liked watching McElhenny run with the ball," he said. "I learned as the years went by that after I made my first block on the line to immediately get up and chase him downfield, because more than likely he was coming back, and I would get an opportunity for another block or a good blindside."

St. Clair found joy in blocking, as the actual act of blocking in the 1950s was much more different than how it's done in the modern game.

"We couldn't use our hands like they can nowadays. Our hands had to be into their chests," he said. "It was a real disadvantage in pass blocking. But I really enjoyed run blocking and making that contact. Leg-whipping was legal in those days. As lineman, I really enjoyed that technique. I used to put shin guards on backwards so I wouldn't hurt my calves."

Against pass rushers like the Colts' Gino Marchetti, it was a real challenge for St. Clair. "He was one of the best defensive ends the game has ever seen. He had a field day if you were trying to block him. He was so quick and he could put his hands on me, but I wasn't allowed to do the same."

But St. Clair had a trick up his sleeve to limit Marchetti's production. "I used to put Vaseline on my jersey so his hands would slip off," he revealed. "I got caught a couple of times, always hoping I wouldn't get caught. If I did, I'd have to go in and take off my jersey and change into a new one."

Despite his unique tactics, St. Clair earned the respect of the entire league for his blocking skills.

In a memorable performance against the Rams in 1959, St. Clair convoyed teammate, Abe Woodson, on a 105-yard kickoff return. Although game films showed that 14 blocks helped clear the way for Woodson, it was St. Clair contributing six of them. His crushing blocks sent a pair of Rams out of the game with injuries.

Besides being a bruising blocker, St. Clair had an impact on the defensive side of the ball, blocking ten kicks in 1956.

"I would line up over the center, and one of the reasons I was able to block so many was because of my height," he pointed out. "I would leapfrog over the center a lot. The first couple of times I would duck my head and plow through the center and run over the top of the blocker with my cleats.

"The next time I looked at the snapper, and instead of him getting turned over backwards again and having my cleats running over his chest, he'd go down automatically on all fours. Once they did that, I'd leapfrog over the top of them, and I could jump straight up, and usually I could block the field goal, extra point, or punt."

Most of the time he was able to cleanly block the ball; however, one time he was the recipient of a swift kick to the face.

"I blocked a punt against the Rams' Van Brocklin, and I knocked the ball away from his foot," St. Clair said. "I was in there so quickly that he kicked me in the teeth. I went over to the sideline and they shoved cotton in my mouth, and until it got so bad I had to take Novocain in my mouth, but I kept playing. I lost five teeth as a result of the play."

In 1957, St. Clair, the team captain, again displayed his unbelievable toughness. After breaking his shoulder in the 49ers' first game of the season, an injury that required surgery, he surprised his teammates with his triumphant return seven weeks later playing against the Giants at Yankee Stadium.

The night before the game, he busted in on the team meeting and he yelled, "Moses has returned from the dead to lead you guys to the Promised Land!"

With St. Clair in the lineup, the 49ers upset the favored Giants, 27-17, as he had a productive day blocking for his teammates, and he was awarded the game ball for his play in his courageous comeback effort.

The victory sparked a three-game winning streak to close out the year, and the team would earn a playoff spot. Their season ultimately ended at home with a 31-27 loss to Detroit. It was the closest that St. Clair and the 49ers came to winning a championship.

It seems unthinkable today, but most players in the early 1950s still required regular jobs in the off-season to support themselves.

After the 1957 season, St. Clair joined up with the 49ers off-season basketball team and played center. They played exhibition games against the Rams, Wilt Chamberlain and the Harlem Globetrotters before sellout crowds. He also auditioned for the role of Tarzan with Paramount Studios while he was still playing for the 49ers.

"I would have won the role, but they couldn't get a rope to hold me, because I was nearly seven feet tall," he said. "The extras were short guys and I looked like Gulliver! Anyway, the role ended up going to a Hollywood actor. I was just too tall."

St. Clair's career extended past the 1950s, however he ruptured his Achilles in 1962 and 1964 and was forced to retire. During his 12-year career with the 49ers, he was All-NFL three times and started in five Pro Bowls. He was as colorful and versatile on the field, as well as off the field.

19

"Oh, What Hands!"

Billy Gene Wilson was the cornerstone of the 49ers offense throughout the 1950s. While not being blessed with great speed, the receiver had reliable hands and a relentless competitive streak. He was willing to pay the price for greatness, personal sacrifice and hard work to go along with his unselfish goals, while helping the welfare and success of his former teammates.

The 49ers had two favorite nicknames for Wilson: the "Goose" and the "Poor Devil." The first one referred to his build at six foot four, 185 pounds, long-necked and resembling a famished man. The other concerned his job because he caught passes that could have risked his life.

During his rookie season of 1951, Wilson suffered an ankle injury in the league opener, missing three games. When he returned from the injury, he was in mid-season form. He showed no sign of any side effects from being out of action, as he once again started to make fantastic catches that had made him one of the most feared receivers in the league.

In 1951, the Lions held a half-game lead over the second-place Rams as the Lions headed west to take on the 49ers in the season finale. At a press luncheon, the Lions head coach, Buddy Parker, was quizzed at length on his preparations for the 49ers:

"You've neglected to mention the man we fear the most," Parker declared. "That Wilson is only a rookie, but he's going to be the best end in the league. Our defensive backs say he's the toughest receiver to cover they've gone up against."

(Author's note: Considering the likes of the Rams' Hirsch and Fears, both Hall of Famers in the league, that was a pretty impressive statement he made.)

It was a prophetic statement by Parker, for the 49ers came up with a tricky maneuver during the game involving Wilson.

Tittle handed the ball off to Perry, who would find the heralded rookie on a 34-yard scoring pass. Wilson's reception was a never-to-be-forgotten catch in the end zone. The play bewildered the Lions, as they failed to recover. The 49ers went on to a 21-17 upset win, thus permitting the Rams to back in to the divisional title.

Wilson was born in Sayre, Oklahoma. His black hair, high cheek-bones and rangy frame bespoke the Fox and Sax Indian blood that coursed through his veins. At age three, his family fled the Dust Bowl drought of the Depression and moved to California, where he grew up in Campbell, California, and was an all-around athlete star at Campbell High.

Typical of his personality, Wilson took a special speed-up course so he could get his diploma six months early and enlist in the Navy during World War II. He served as a signalman on a patrol craft in the South Pacific.

After the war, Wilson enrolled at San Jose State in the fall of 1947. As a junior, he was already noted as one of the school's most memorable football and basketball players.

He reported to the 49ers in July of 1951, as he had been a "red shirt" 22nd draft choice the year before, and he had another year of college eligibility remaining.

On the first day of practice, Wilson met Y. A. Tittle. The pair put on a clinic that displayed both players' unique abilities, wowing the onlookers in the process as the 49ers had uncovered a masterful aerial combination.

"He was one of the fiercest competitors I ever played with," said Tittle. "He was my number-one receiver. When I needed a big catch, I went to him because I knew he would make the play."

Albert said of Wilson: "In all my years of football—high school, college, and professional—Wilson was one of the greatest competitors I've ever seen. He was one of the most underrated players on the team. He had hands of glue and could really go up for the ball. His ability to run after the catch was amazing. He was a super guy, so congenial, humble, and a nice person."

Wilson had many personal thrills during his football career with the 49ers; one came following the 1955 season as he was voted MVP of the 1956 Pro Bowl based on these numbers: he caught 11 passes for 154 yards in leading the Western Conference to a 26-19 victory.

His entire 10-year career was spent with the 49ers as he finished with 407 catches for 5,902 yards and 49 touchdowns.

His other accomplishments included earning first team All-Pro in 1957, playing in six consecutive Pro Bowl, placing fourth in touchdown catches, fifth in receiving yards and sixth in receptions in franchise history. He also ranks fourth among the 49ers receiving touchdown leaders and sixth with 15.5 yards per catch.

His statistics were all the more impressive, considering they were achieved in 12-game seasons and before a series of NFL rules changes opened up the passing game. Wilson was one of the few players of the 1950s era who would excel today. When he hung up his cleats following the 1960 season, only the Packers' Don Hutson had more receptions.

20

Interview with "The Jet"

Fullback Joe "The Jet" Perry was one of four members of the 49ers "Million Dollar Backfield" to make the Pro Football Hall of Fame. His career rushing statistics of 7,344 yards is second in the records book, while his 50 rushing touchdowns are tied for the top spot in the record books.

I have vivid memories of "The Jet" from games I saw him play in person as he set many records. In 2009, I had the chance to sit down with Perry before a 49ers game and express my gratitude to him for all the great memories he bestowed on me. In return, he answered questions about his career that spanned 14 seasons with the 49ers.

MARTIN JACOBS: Did you want to play football for a living?

JOE PERRY: "Not at first. In high school and college, I had majored in math and got A's in calculus and advanced trigonometry, as I planned to become an electrical engineer after I graduated."

MJ: Where did you play football in high school?

JP: I played at David Starr Jordon High in Los Angeles.

MJ: I heard where your mother was against it.

JP: She refused to sign the release, which would absolve the school of any responsibility in case of injury. So, without her knowledge I signed it for her. Ironically, the first day of practice I broke my ankle. Later I was confronted by my mother with the forgery, but I later convinced her to let me play after the injury healed. I started for the varsity football team as a 13-year-old."

MJ: Did you play college ball?

JP: My heart was set on attending UCLA, so that I could follow in the footsteps of my idol, Kenny Washington, as I had the academic and athletic accomplishments to qualify, but I was snubbed by the University. It seemed they weren't ready for "black" football players. So, I played at Compton Junior College.

MJ: Did you set any records at Compton?

JP: I went on to set a school scoring record with 114 points in 1944. But after one season at Compton, I enlisted in the Navy.

MJ: Did you play any other sports in college?

JP: I ran track, high jumped and long jumped. I also was a good baseball player and even better softball player. On Saturday nights I loved to bowl.

MJ: How fast were you?

JP: I won the 100-yard dash in 9.7 seconds at Compton, and I finished second to Mel Patton, the former Olympian, in 9.4.

MJ: Tell me about the Navy.

JP: I had just turned 17 when I joined the Navy. I served on an LST in the Pacific until the war ended. I was a coxswain. I finished up my military obligation at the Alameda Naval Air Station, decommissioning ships and pulling up anchor chains for the Navy. When I wasn't playing football for them, I was a pitcher and we won the All-Navy softball tournament.

MJ: Didn't you receive any scholarships?

JP: After three years in the Navy, I received scholarship offers from Washington, Oregon, USC, Nevada and Columbia of the Ivy League. At the time I was married with a child, so it came down to using my G.I Bill from the Navy, or play pro football.

MJ: So you signed with the 49ers?

JP: While playing football for the NAS Hellcats, my football exploits attracted both the Rams from the NFL and the 49ers from the All-America Football Conference. Shaw and Albert scouted me in a game against a service team. That day I scored three touchdowns.

Though the Rams offered me $5,000 more than the 49ers, I signed a contract with San Francisco the following day. I still had 10 months left in the Navy before my discharge from the service before I could join the team.

MJ: Why did you pick the 49ers?

JP: I chose the 49ers because of my immediate bond with the owner, Tony Morabito. He was like a second father to me.

MJ: Do you remember your first play as a 49er?

JP: Yes, I ran 58 yards for a touchdown against the Buffalo Bills. That was in 1948.

MJ: Weren't you the "King" before McElhenny?

JP: Not many people know this. I was the "King" before Mac came. Albert named both of us the "King." Then McElhenny came on the scene in 1952, and he took over the crown as the "King." I was re-named the "Little King."

MJ: So how did you become "The Jet"?

JP: As time progressed, my quickness and speed earned me the new nickname the "Jet," again from Albert. That stayed with me until to the end of my career.

MJ: What was your playing weight throughout your career?

JP: Between 195 and 207.

MJ: How was your running style different from McElhenny's?

JP: I was ultraconservative and never took gambles. I moved straight ahead and seldom veered from my course and fought for every inch. Hugh was a guy who would sacrifice 10 yards to look for daylight.

MJ: Who was the faster, you or Hugh?

JP: No one ever questioned my speed, but at 50 yards, I would say I was slightly faster. At 100 yards, I would pick McElhenny.

MJ: Some say you had the quickest start.

JP: Coach Shaw put a stopwatch on me and found that I could start three yards behind the line of scrimmage line, take a handoff from Albert, and get through the hole in six-tenths of a second. He once said I ran like a bowling ball fired from a howitzer going straight down the middle, sending pins flying in every direction.

MJ: Who had the most carries?

JP: I guess I did. It seemed I either carried the ball or plunged into the line on a fake most every play. I also plunged on a fake on at least 50 percent of 49ers' pass plays. I ran so fast and faked well that most linebackers were told to tackle me every time I popped through the line.

MJ: What was the "Perry Trap" play?

JP: It was a maneuver which our coach developed for me. The only difference between the "Perry Trap" and an ordinary one was that our big tackle St. Clair crossed over from the other side and usually flattened a linebacker as I plunged through the hole.

MJ: What was it like being the first black player for the 49ers?

JP: There definitely was some racial prejudice shown towards me on the field. I always was patient with those who spoke badly about me, but I would not tolerate any physical punishment because of my race. I would retaliate immediately if I believed my physical well-being was being compromised. It made me very much respected among my teammates. We were like a family and race relations were quite good.

MJ: Did you suffer any major injuries in your career?

JP: Yes. As my injuries mounted in college I was referred to "the man most carried off the field" in Compton Junior College history. In my first seven seasons as a 49er, from 1948 to 1955, I broke three ribs, lost nine teeth, suffered two shoulder separations, sprained my ankle nine times, sprained my knee three times, tore ligaments in my legs twice, and I had 27 stitches taken in my face.

MJ: What was the worst injury?

JP: One hot day against the Rams, I think in 1954, I tossed aside the helmet that had a fitted mask for me, for one without a mask. Three plays later I got elbowed by Ram's Larry Brink, who knocked out nine of my teeth—six molars and three from a bridge I had fitted after a game against the Steelers. Still, I scored three touchdowns that day.

MJ: So how much did it cost the insurance company?

JP: Only $320. After all, extractions weren't necessary (Perry said laughing).

MJ: Was that the last injury in your career?

JP: No. In the infamous playoff game of the 1957 season, I fractured my zeugmatic bone in the third quarter. One side of my face was caved in, but I didn't come out of the game. Despite the pleas of my teammates to seek medical attention, I played on."

MJ: What were your best seasons with the 49ers?

JP: I think the 1953 and 1954 seasons. I had consecutive 1,000-yard rushing seasons at a time when that specific statistic truly was a fantastic feat. Just to be the first NFL back to do it in back-to-back seasons was an accomplishment.

MJ: Did you play any other position besides fullback?

JP: At the start of the 1954 season, I filled in as placekicker for Soltau, who was injured. I kicked five points after touchdowns in the opener, a 41-7 win over the Redskins. And the following week, I added another PAT and a 14-yard field goal against the Rams, until Soltau returned in the second half in a 24-24 tie. I was never asked to kick again.

MJ: What do you remember most about the "Million Dollar Backfield"?

JP: If not for McElhenny's season-ending injury in 1954, all three of us, Mac, John Henry and I might have finished 1-2-3 in NFL rushing, not sure in what order. That would have been a league first, three backs from one team. As it turned out, Johnson ended up second to me in the final NFL rushing stats.

MJ: Did you guys really make a million dollars?

JP: That's a joke (Joe said laughing). If you put all of our salaries together, it didn't amount to that. It was our GM Lou Spadia who said we played like we were worth a million dollars.

MJ: Was there a Joe Perry day?

JP: Yes. On August 28, 1955, the 49ers honored me at Kezar before our game with Cleveland. Norm Standlee was the emcee. I was the first black player in the NFL to be saluted in such a fashion. It was a humbling experience. I got a TV set and furniture for my house. Fans thought I got a car because there was a Pontiac on the field. But I worked for Boas Pontiac in the off season, who put the car out there."

MJ: I heard you had a radio show.

JP: During the 1950s, I was given my own radio show five days a week from 4 to 6 p.m., on station KLX in Oakland. I spun records and interviewed my 49er teammates and celebrities like Dinah Washington."

MJ: Why did you leave the 49ers?

JP: I left the 49ers by my own choice in 1961 for the Baltimore Colts. I felt that I could no longer co-exist with head coach Red Hickey, who refused to play me in most of the games in 1960.

MJ: But you came back to the 49ers in 1963.

JP: After two seasons in Baltimore, the Colts cut me. Vic Morabito called me and asked me to come home and retire as a 49er. My loyalty to the Morabito family was too powerful a pull, though. So, I returned for one last season.

MJ: Any regrets Joe?

JP: I always believed that my two years, 1948 and 1949, in the All-America Football Conference, that my statistics should have been included with my overall NFL accomplishments. The competition was just as good as the ones in the NFL. The Browns proved that by beating the Rams in the 1950 NFL championship, after barely beating us in the AAFC title game 21-7 in 1949.

21

Moegle to Maegle

Until his name came up during a TV special honoring sports heroes, Dickey Moegle, oops, make that Maegle, (he changed the spelling of his last name after retirement) was a name that hadn't crossed my mind in decades.

Back in the 1950s, I would see him play in at least six to eight games a season for the 49ers. This allowed me to get acquainted with him on the field after a game.

I do recall he was friendly, and he could not help signing an autograph for a kid. I was 11 years of age in December of 1954, when for the first time I had seen Moegle perform in the Shriner's East-West game at Kezar Stadium.

In the slush that day, Moegle wore No. 47, the same number he wore at Rice University and with the 49ers. In that game, he gained 36 yards on seven carries and returned three punts for 28 yards. Once the game concluded, I left my seat, hopped the railing, and dashed onto the field toward Moegle. When I approached him, I asked him for his chin strap. Moegle said, "Sure, why not?"

He proceeded to rip off the leather chin strap from his helmet and handed it to me. I then followed him to the east end of the stadium until we reached the players' tunnel. From there he disappeared into palpable darkness.

I enjoyed Moegle's unmeasured candor and meeting an All-American, who at the time was perhaps the most heavily coveted college player in the nation.

While playing for Rice, located in Houston, Texas, Moegle's credentials were well documented during his three years on the varsity. The mark of an Owls' team of that era was its ability to attract players, whose intellect matched their athletic skills. Moegle was one of them.

It is unfortunate that in national circles he is best remembered for being blindsided by Alabama's Tommy Lewis, who came off the bench to tackle Moegle, who had broken clear and headed for the goal line. That it happened before a national TV audience during the 1954 Cotton Bowl game gave that play a life of its own.

"I wanted to be doggone sure I didn't kick up any chalk and get called for stepping out of bounds because no one was going to catch me. I just caught sight of this guy crouching down and I remember thinking, why is he coming out on the field, then like...Pow!!...he really cracked me and down I went," Moegle said modestly.

That illegal and potentially injurious infraction put the spotlight on Lewis, who had an otherwise insignificant game and away from Moegle, whose 265 rushing yards was a Cotton Bowl rushing record that stood for 54 years.

Lewis enjoyed the resulting limelight while making a round of TV talk shows and media interviews. Moegle, who fortunately was not injured on the play, landed on the Ed Sullivan show the following day.

"All in all," stated Moegle, "I remained quiet." But after prodding around a while admitted, "It bugged the hell out of me!" I could not blame him.

His senior year was 1954, and he would finish his college career as the nation's fourth leading rusher with 906 yards, an average of 6.2 yards per carry. In addition, he would finish as the top punt returner, returning 15 kicks 293 yards, an average of 19.5.

A 91-yard return against Baylor in the season finale was a highlight for the future 49er.

He would be selected by the 49ers with their first-round pick in 1955, 10th overall to play in the NFL. When he arrived in San Francisco, the 49ers were in transition. Norman "Red" Strader had replaced the immortal Buck Shaw.

With the 49ers, Moegle would be seeing plenty of "red" in the near future. The team was in desperate need of help in the secondary. He was looking to fit the mold.

"I told the coach I'd play any position he wanted. If you pay me, I'll play it," said an enthusiastic Moegle.

Just a month into his first season, Moegle had his chance to show off his accreditations as a defensive back, offensive back, safety on kickoff and punt returns—all in one game— against the Lions at Briggs Stadium.

"That day I played everywhere on the field. McElhenny was nursing a foot injury, so I was getting time at halfback, and I caught a 25-yard pass from Tittle—my first catch as a 49er. Just a few plays later, I was able to turn the corner on a 10-yard sweep and run it into the end zone for my first touchdown as a 49er.

"Later I returned a kickoff 61 yards to set up another score. We ended up beating a championship-caliber team in the Lions. From then on, I worked my way up to a starter," said Moegle.

Although Moegle lasted just five seasons with the club, his finest season came on defense in 1957 when he had eight interceptions as he was selected first-team All-Pro by the New York News.

From 1955-59, Moegle had 28 career interceptions and accumulated 305 rushing yards and six touchdowns as a 49er.

In the team's fourth game of the 1958 season, he would go down with a season-ending knee injury. This injury would cause him to be less productive in 1959.

Thus, Moegle was traded to the Steelers for a No. 1 draft pick. In turn, the 49ers chose UCLA's All-American halfback, Jimmy Johnson, who played 16 years with the 49ers and ended up in the NFL Hall of Fame.

Ironically, my second conversation with Moegle was at a Chamber of Commerce luncheon held for present and past 49ers players at the Palace Hotel in San Francisco in 1959. I told Moegle that I saw him play in the East-West Shriner's game, and I had become a fan of his. He was gracious and gave me a pat on my shoulder.

Two things have changed since I first met Moegle. After his retirement from football, he changed the spelling of his name from Moegle to Maegle, because he said it sounded better, and secondly, he turned out to be a very good pro football player.

22

End of an Era

This book would not be complete unless I devoted some credit to the 49ers' only championship appearance as members of the AAFC against the Browns on December 11, 1949, in Cleveland, Ohio.

The 49ers (10-3) and the Browns (10-1-2) would meet to settle the league's fourth and final championship. It was only fitting that two of the league's finest would battle for the final conference championship trophy as they would also represent, not only their league, but in all of professional football.

A rivalry as deep-seated and intense between of these two great teams would need no additional incentives to insure a terrific struggle in this title game. But this was no other game. For fans this was a "players' game"...the "rubber game"...the "championship game." Pride as well as the "crown" was also at stake.

Earlier in the season, the 49ers came up with a new slogan: "The 49ers in '49." This was the slogan they had hoped to be reality, until the last meeting between these two foes.

The Browns, maybe envious and proud of their 1948 championship title, were determined to repeat, ending as the only team to hoist all four of the trophies. The Browns' dominance of the league's title games was most evident, playing against three different opponents in the four games, winning by an average of 18 points per title game.

Beginning in 1946, the 49ers' inaugural season, the two teams would meet eight times with the Browns holding a two-win margin, 8-6, and by the margin of a field goal on the scoreboard, 27-24. The 49ers won their first matchup of the perennial AAFC rivals, 34-20, but the Browns won the return engagement, 14-7. On the road to winning the 1947-48 AAFC titles, the Browns won four straight contests against the 49ers that included a pair of 14-7 contests, a rout of 37-14, and taking a 31-28 thriller.

Entering into the 1949 contest, the two teams had a combined record of 9-1. But in 1949, the 49ers (4-1) would give the undefeated Browns (5-0) a fancy 56-28 drubbing at Kezar in front of a full house of 59,000 bulging at the seams. The club estimated it had to return orders for another 40,000 tickets.

The Browns entered the contest without tasting defeat in 31 consecutive games, so it was considered a monumental upset. Legendary college football coach, Glenn S. "Pop" Warner who viewed the game from the press box told the writers: "On this day, the 49ers were the greatest football team I have ever seen!"

A few weeks later, the Browns avenged the loss against the 49ers with a 30-28 decision as Lou Groza's 38-yard field goal late in the fourth quarter clinched the triumph for the Ohio team.

The 1949 statistics proved how evenly these teams were matched: Joe Perry's 783 yards was the tops on the team that had compiled 4,793 total yards, compared to that of Marion Motley of Cleveland, who compiled 570 yards of his team's 4,611 yards. On the ground, the 49ers had more than 1,000 yardage difference (2,798 yards to 1,782), but the Browns' strength was through the air. Their field general Otto Graham was supreme with 2,929 passing yards against Frankie Albert's 1,195.

Graham led in total offense and passing, Perry in rushing, Albert in punting, Max Speedie in receiving, and Alyn Beals in scoring. In addition, the 49ers' Jimmy Cason led in punt returns. This all added up to the two best teams in the AAFC. So the game was on.

Prior to the big game, the 49ers had lost one of their top rushers in John Strzykalski to a broken leg and defensive back Paul Carr suffered a career-ending knee injury.

Still, the Browns and 49ers were set to renew the Graham, Albert, Motley, Perry, and the Speedy, Beals rivalries. This sextet represented the finest performers the AAFC had to offer. Their play and records had dominated the league statistics in 1949 as they had in the past.

The 49ers, with visions of a huge crowd and lucrative shares of the gate, arrived in Cleveland a few days before the big game and were greeted with a snow storm.

Only 22,550 Browns' faithful fans showed up to watch the Browns win a lopsided 21-7 game. Just a year earlier, these teams drew over 82,000 at Cleveland's Municipal Stadium. It wasn't a great game for the spectators to watch in the snow, slush and wind.

Although the field conditions were less than ideal, the elements made for a slippery field, at least for the visitors. Perry would only manage 36 yards on six carries, while Motley was able to keep his footing rolling at top speed.

The Browns had the game under control from the onset. Halfback Dub "Special Delivery" Jones drove over the left guard for the first touchdown in the early minutes of the game which set the tone for the entire game. He would also make the final play of the first half, a four-yard gain to the San Francisco 25.

The fans would only rise to their feet once, as when Motley flashed his lightning bolt speed on a 63-yard scamper in the third quarter, scoring his team's second touchdown. Jones would score, not only the Browns' final touchdown, but it would also be the last one in the history of the AAFC in league play.

Following the ensuing kickoff, the 49ers moved the ball down the field, churning out 73 yards on less than ideal conditions. Albert's scoring strike to end Paul Salata from 24 yards away provided the lone score for the visitors. Only one other time did the 49ers threaten, and that was in the second quarter when they marched to Cleveland's 24.

The drive was stalled following Horace Gillom's 10-yard sack of Albert on third down. Joe Ventrano's attempted 41-yard field goal failed to add to the 49ers' afternoon tally.

The Browns' Graham completed only 7 of 17 for 128 yards, but three of them came at vital points. He connected on a long one to Speedie for 38 yards in the first touchdown drive, and then twice connected with Dante Lavelli on completions of 23 and 10 yards as the Browns marched towards the end zone for their last points.

Graham also contributed to his team's rushing stats: nine carries as he picked-up 62 yards. But the most amazing part of the game was the work of Cleveland's defensive unit. It held the 49ers' ground attack to 122 yards and would all but stop Albert's aerial game as he would only complete nine of his 24 attempts.

The 49er backs spent most of the game trying to unravel themselves from the embrace of Cleveland's linemen. One of the defense gems of the battle was Browns' defensive back Warren Lahr's effort on an Albert pass to Salata in the third period. Lahr knocked the ball out of his reach just as the 49er end was about to make the catch for what would have been a sure touchdown. This defensive job even drew praise from Salata himself. He patted Warren on the back as he returned upfield.

The Browns won the game and remained as champions, the only champions the league ever knew.

For its final AAFC championship, each Cleveland player received $266.11, while each 49er player, $172.61. Even though the AAFC would fold, three of its teams, San Francisco, Cleveland and Baltimore, would live on and become part of the NFL the following season.

23

49ers' Curtain Call

The final game in the history of the AAFC occurred on December 17, 1949 at Rice Stadium in Houston, Texas. It was billed as the Shamrock Charity Bowl All-Star Game in which the 49ers were mighty contributors. Up until then, the NFL and the AAFC had fought a nasty bidding war for players from both leagues, but the sides had called a truce on December 11, 1949, when they announced a merger.

The Browns and 49ers, along with the Colts, would all be merged into the NFL for the 1950 season. The other AAFC teams followed: the Buffalo Bills merged with the Browns, the New York Yankees were split among the New York Giants and the New York Bulldogs in the NFL, and the Los Angeles Dons mixed with the Los Angeles Rams. The only team left out in the cold was the Chicago Rockets who were disbanded.

Glenn "Diamond Glenn" McCarthy, a Houston oil tycoon, announced that he would sponsor an All-Star Game as a charity event to raise money for Holly Hall (Home for the Aged) of Houston.

McCarthy dreamed of Houston being a professional football town, and he had been tentatively assured of a new franchise by the

AAFC, but that promise faded away with the merger. His Shamrock Bowl would give the community exposure and expose the community to professional football.

As it turned out, it was McCarthy's Shamrock Bowl that would be the last curtain call for the AAFC.

The game would pit the 1949 Champion Browns against a team of all-Stars selected from the other six AAFC franchises. An imposing array of talent was picked for the game. The Browns qualified by defeating the 49ers, and they boasted perhaps the greatest team in the history of the AAFC to that point.

They went 9-1-2 in 1949 and were led by quarterback Otto Graham and coached by the legendary Paul Brown. The All-Stars were led by rookie sensation, Y. A. Tittle from the Colts and quarterback Frankie Albert, fullback Joe Perry, defensive back Jimmy Cason, end Alyn Beals, and guard Visco Grgich, all from the 49ers. The All-Stars were coached by Red Strader of the Yankees, who had lost a semifinal playoff game to the 49ers a few weeks earlier.

Three days after winning the final AAFC Championship Game, the Browns arrived in Houston by rail on December 14. The city of Houston was so focused on the game that the newspaper, the Chronicle headline following the AAFC championship read: "Browns Brush Aside 49ers to Qualify for Bowl Game."

For a pricey sum of $15 ($5 end-zone seats), patrons were treated to the game and entertainment provided by radio stars Jack Benny, Phil Harris (who starred on the Jack Benny Show), and Dinah Shore, which preceded the 2 p.m. kickoff.

The three entertained the crowd of 12,000 in a downpour. The fans, although small in number, were very enthusiastic about the game. The first 10 minutes was a mud brawl as neither team threatened. Late in the first period, starting on his own 32-yard line, the

49ers' Albert led the Stars on a 16-play drive that brought the game its first score.

Albert mixed in passing and running plays that resulted in the tally. He connected with fellow All-Stars Chet Mutryn (Buffalo) and Lamar Davis (Colts), as the drive reached the Cleveland 26-yard line.

The Yankees' Otto Schnenbacher hauled in a pass from the left-handed Albert, placing the ball at the 15. Now it was time for the ground game to take over. Runs by New York's Buddy Young and the 49ers' Perry split the 10 yards, giving the Stars a first and goal at the four-yard line.

From there Mutryn carried twice for the score, barreling into the end zone from the two-yard line with the clock showing 1:30 to play in the opening quarter. Albert missed the extra point, leaving the score at 6-0.

The All-Stars' defense would hold the league's four-time champion Browns in check for most of the second quarter before finding the end zone for the go-ahead score. Graham hit Dub Jones with a flair pass at the five and the receiver did the rest. Following Groza's PAT, the Browns took a 7-6 advantage.

On the ensuing kickoff, the All-Stars surmounted a 91-yard drive on 12 plays behind Albert's passing and the running of Young. The big play of the drive came from the Browns' 26 when Young shrugged off a tackle, sprinted to his right and took the ball 23 yards to the Cleveland 13.

On the All-Stars' next possession, a two-yard loss, the team would start its next and last scoring drive of the game. Albert escaped pressure from the Browns' defensive unit, finding Buffalo's Al Baldwin at the five-yard marker, who would then scamper into the end zone for a 25-yard touchdown.

The extra point was again missed, but the it didn't affect the game's final tally as the All-Stars would take the 12-7 margin into the locker room, leaving it up to the defense to keep the Browns off the scoreboard.

Adverse conditions in the second half would keep both teams from adding to the first half's scoring. In the mud, the Browns would threaten three times during the final quarter of play, only to be turned away by a stout defensive stand each time.

Two picks by Cason of the 49ers added to the pressure defense that Graham faced all day. The All-Star defense would sack Graham for losses totaling 55 yards for the day, thus keeping the halftime score of 12-7 as the final tally. This would be only the fifth loss in Cleveland's franchise history.

Statistical standouts for the winners came from a pair of 49ers and a future teammate. Albert of the 49ers completed 6 of 13 for 70 yards and Perry rushed for 57 yards, while Tittle, (who would join up with the 49ers in 1951) was 7 of 15 passes for 66 yards.

"It was one of the great memories of my life. We were treated like movie stars," said Tittle.

In retrospect of the last AAFC game, it saw the 49ers' stars emerge who were able to show their abilities, proving their worth and their talent were not just limited to that of the AAFC, but they were ready to take on a bigger challenge playing in the NFL starting in 1950.

24

John Brodie: College All-Star

For more than 40 years, beginning in 1934, the annual Chicago College All-Star Game was played at the beginning of each August at Soldier Field in Chicago. The game was a fan favorite while helping establish the NFL as a premier sports league. At the forefront of the Golden Age, the players were often seen as mercenaries while the college players were better known and more popular across the country.

Arch Ward, the sports editor for the Chicago Tribune, who was instrumental in helping Tony Morabito gain an AAFC franchise for San Francisco, cultivated the idea of hosting an annual game between the defending NFL Champions and the best of the recently graduated college football stars.

And though the NFL stars usually finished on top, the game remained competitive throughout the 1950s. It also continued to grow in popularity among college and NFL fans in the Chicago area. With TV coverage of football still in its infancy, the game provided a rare opportunity for fans to see some greats who rarely made appearances in certain areas.

In 1947 the largest crowd of 105,840—the most ever to attend a pro football game in the U.S.—watched the College All-Stars shut-out the defending NFL champions Chicago Bears, 17-0. Attendance remained above 88,000 until 1955.

Over time the NFL teams would become stronger, thus the game would become less competitive. After winning eight times between 1934 and 1958, the All-Stars claimed only one win over the final 17 games in the series.

On August 9, 1957, the 22-year-old quarterback, John Brodie, who played for Stanford and was the 49ers' No. 1 draft pick in the first round (No. 3 overall), would be named the starting quarterback for the All-Stars.

In his first try against the powerhouse World Champion New York Giants, Brodie looked to be much more than an amateur, until the last few minutes in a delayed contest played amid rain storms.

The opening kickoff of the game was delayed 12 minutes, and the second-half kickoff was delayed another 22 minutes. In spite of the soggy field, Brodie motored the All-Stars downfield in the opening quarter.

After Illinois's Wayne Bock recovered Alex Webster's fumble at the All-Stars' 45-yard line, Brodie engineered a 55-yard drive in 11 plays for a touchdown and a 7-0 All-Star's advantage.

His passes were sharp and accurate. His first toss was an 11-yarder to USC's halfback, Jon Arnett, and his next toss was a 19-yarder to Michigan's end, Ron Kramer, who gave the All-Stars a first down at the Giants 25.

From that point, an old-fashioned Pop Warner double-reverse broke Abe Woodson, the speedster from Illinois and 49ers' No. 2 draft pick, around the left end for 18 yards to the Giants' seven-yard line. Arnett added another five yards, until halfback Billy Ray Barnes fumbled, and Mike Sandusky (Maryland) recovered the ball at the four-yard line. A penalty against the Giants moved the ball to the two, half the distance to the goal line, but the going got tougher for the All-Stars. Brodie threw two incomplete passes and Arnett was held to no gain.

With the Giants expecting another pass from Brodie, Barnes cracked the middle of the Giants line on a plunge play and scored. Paul Hornung's (Notre Dame) kick for the extra point went wide. The All-Stars looked like champions on that drive with Brodie at the helm.

The Giants countered with a 32-yard field goal, cutting the All-Stars' lead to 6-3. They added another touchdown scored by Ken McAfee on a 38-yard toss from George Conerly in the second quarter. Brodie then guided the All-Stars 85 yards in 12 plays, culminating in a Paige Cothern 12-yard field goal to end the half with New York in front 10-9, and they never looked back.

Brodie, who was knocked out late in the second quarter was back, fresh as ever, for the second half. From then on the Giants had it pretty much their way as they extended their lead to 17-9 in the fourth quarter. Brodie got his team close enough for Cothern's second field goal from 33 yards out, cutting the Giants lead to 17-9.

The Giants added a field goal and a safety by way of a Woodson fumble on a double-reverse attempt, in which he was tackled in the end zone by the Giants' Dick Nolan. New York held off one last All-Star threat to win the game.

Final score: New York Giants 22, College All-Stars 12.

Brodie was named the game's MVP. He completed 9 of 20 passes for 94 yards, and he remained upbeat about his performance.

"I think I played well. I just could not get away back there. When the rain came, I was stuck in the mud. The ball felt like a watermelon to me. We were going good in the second quarter, but then it started to rain again. With a little luck, we might have won this one," said a modest Brodie.

NFL Hall of Fame quarterback, Otto Graham, who coached the College All-Stars, said after the game, "Brodie was one of the finest quarterbacks I had ever seen."

Brodie would report to the 49ers' training camp in Moraga the following day to begin his career with the team. Other 49ers who performed for the College All-Stars (1950-59) included:

1950: Leo Nomellini, T (Minnesota)

Don Campora, T (College of Pacific)

1951: Pete Schabarum, HB (California)

Dick Sterre, T (Drake)

1952: Bill Carey, E (Michigan State)

Pat O'Donahue, E (Wisconsin)

Marion Campbell, T (Georgia)

Bob Toneff, T (Notre Dame)

Hugh McElhenny, HB (Washington)

1953: Hal Miller, T (Georgia Tech)

George Morris, C (Georgia Tech)

1954: Morreau Williams, G (TCU)

Bobby Hantla, G (Kansas)

1955: Matt Hazeltine, C (California)

Sam Palumbo, G (Notre Dame)

Frank Morze, C (Boston College)

Dickey Moegle, HB (Rice)

1956: Bill Herchman, T (Texas Tech)

Bruce Bosley, T (West Virginia)

Earl Morrall, QB (Michigan State)

1957: John Brodie, QB (Stanford)

Abe Woodson, HB (Illinois)

Mike Sandusky, T (Maryland)

Jim Ridlon, HB (Syracuse)

1958: Jimmy Pace, HB (Michigan)

Charley Krueger, T (Texas A&M)

Billy Atkins, HB (Auburn)

1959: Dave Baker, HB (Oklahoma)

Dan James, C (Ohio State)

Eddie Dove, HB (Colorado)

Frank Germania, T (Notre Dame)

25

Follies at Kezar

On August 10, 1952, the 49ers hit a milestone at Kezar, scoring 79 unanswered points in an exhibition game against the San Francisco Broncos.

The Broncos were a semi-pro team from our City with a roster of 28, which included former players from the University of San Francisco, St. Mary's and Santa Clara, and some with no college experience, including a high schooler. Even with an ex-49er, Ed Ballati, appearing their roster, their collection of players was not much of a match for the 49ers.

This was a game to take place of the annual "Reds vs. Blues" intra-squad game that was played with the hope of reducing injuries to the 49ers' players. A year earlier during the intra-squad game, defensive back Jim Cason suffered a pinched nerve in his shoulder and three other players were put out of action for the entire NFL season.

As expected the game was more of a dress rehearsal for the 49ers' upcoming season instead of a game being of competitive nature, or for that matter, a full scrimmage in front of 8,700 fans—not counting the seagulls—who witnessed a sneak peek of their favorite football team.

For the first six minutes of action, which was nothing more than a warm-up, there was a semblance of the fall sport on the emerald green turf of Kezar Stadium. The score was deadlocked at zero. It seemed the Broncos came to play football against a talented 49ers' team.

Over the next two and half hours, the 49ers went on a scoring rampage, putting up 10 touchdowns on the scoreboard. In between, there were a few spots of brilliance, quite a bit of comedy and a great deal of sentiment generated for the underdogs.

Perhaps there would have been even more of everything, if the minute hand on the clock hadn't been surreptitiously moved up two and three minutes at a whack during the third and fourth quarters, by merciful agreement between rival coaches.

Except for the mad dreamers and the uninformed, 49ers' head coach, Buck Shaw, did quite a bit of experimenting against the Broncos. Most provoking to the crowd in the stands, as it was to tackle Leo Nomellini, who had insisted to Coach Shaw to allow the teams' star tackle to move to fullback.

After a few carries of the football, Nomellini was the first to admit, "I've a new respect for backfield men." He grinned. "But remember, I never played the position, with no idea of what the play assignments were. I even had to be told where to move my feet."

Nomellini carried the ball just three times, ponderously and with a fierce expression, gaining a total of three net yards. He then wanted a crack at pass receiver, and on his first try he missed a short toss in the flat from quarterback Jimmy Powers. He was so incensed from dropping the ball, he picked up the nearest Bronco, Bob Daigle, and slammed him to the turf.

The next time Powers had to wait nearly 20 seconds until Nomellini could trundle 30 yards downfield, while stumbling over a defensive back en route to the ball. The pass was accurate, but he misjudged it and it sailed into the hands of a Bronco safety for the lone interception against the 49ers. That was the last time he played receiver.

Shaw wasn't quite sure whether the Broncos game did the club any good or not from a technical aspect. "What can you learn from an afternoon like that?" he wondered. "It was more like basketball scoring than anything."

26

Fort Ord Warriors

The public acceptance for this intriguing game, both in the City and in the outlying communities of Northern California, indicated that a matchup played between the 49ers and the Fort Ord service team would be a spectacular event. It also would be the homecoming for San Francisco native, Ollie Matson.

Matson was a former University of San Francisco All-American and the Chicago Cardinals' No. 1 draft pick in 1952. He played for Fort Ord in 1953 and 1954 and set numerous military scoring records in his brief stay at the Army base.

Fort Ord was then one of the largest U.S. Army bases on the West Coast and had one of the top military football teams in the nation in 1954, as they were known as the Warriors.

The team was made up of several players with both NFL and college experience. In fact, the team would only experience one single game setback, which came a week prior at the hands of the Los Angeles Rams, 7-0.

In the 1953 New Year's Day Poinsettia Bowl against the second best service team, the Quantico Marines, Fort Ord came away with a convincing 55-19 victory. Matson scored three touchdowns with 47- and 48-yard runs and an 18-yard pass from Don Heinrich.

A week later in the Salad Bowl played in Phoenix, the Warriors would trash Great Lakes, another service team, 67-12. Fort Ord's outstanding play would not go unnoticed. The great sports columnist Grantland Rice had called the base team "the best non-professional team ever assembled."

The Fort Ord backfield of Matson and Dave Mann were a powerful 1-2 scoring punch with a formidable quarterback in Jimmy Powers (49ers). They were anchored on defense by big, 300-pound Earl Putnam and ends Dewey Brundage and Cliff Livingston. Football connoisseurs should recognize many of these NFL stars who adorned the Fort Ord uniform from that era:

PLAYER	HEIGHT	WEIGHT	POSITION	NFL TEAM
Ollie Matson	6' 2"	220	HB	Cardinals
Don Heinrich	6' 0"	180	QB	Giants
Earl Putnam	6' 6"	300	T	Rams
Don Burroughs	6' 4"	185	QB	Rams
Sam Baker	6' 0"	215	FB	Redskins
Dewey Brundage	6' 3"	210	E	Steelers
Rudy Bukich	6' 1"	192	QB	Bears
Paul Cameron	6' 1"	195	HB	Steelers
Charles Grant	6' 5"	265	C	Packers
Jim Dublinski	6' 1"	220	C	Redskins
Ron Miller	6' 4"	210	E	Rams
Robert Pevian	6' 1"	230	T	Giants
Jimmy Powers	6' 0"	190	QB	49Ers
Gerald Perry	6' 4"	235	T	Lions
Ed Henke	6' 4"	220	E	49ers
David Mann	6' 1"	190	HB	Cardinals
Cliff Livingston	6' 1"	215	E	Giants
Patterson Cannamela	5' 10"	210	G	Texans

The teams met on an overcast summer day on August 15, 1954, as 19,864 enthused fans filed into Kezar. Also taking in the action were a dozen chartered buses full of soldiers from the base ready to support their fellow troops.

This game would be an epic moment in the history of the franchise, not to mention a true test against a 49er 11 that had the top offense in the Western Conference of the NFL during the 1953 season, which saw the team finish with a 9-3-0 record.

While sitting in the end zone with my Dad, citing the stats of my favorite team came second nature to me. I knew all the 49ers' players by their first name, and I could tell you how many yards that Hugh had gained in 1953. And the same went for the percentage of passes that Y. A. completed or the number of tosses hauled in by Gordy during the previous season.

They were all there stored in my memory bank or on the tip of my tongue, ready to share with anyone who would listen or not. I knew the stats of all of the 49ers.

The game kicked off at 1 p.m., and the 49ers quickly put up 28 points and the 49ers put up 28 points by the end of the first quarter. From then on, Fort Ord matched the 49ers score for score. For a true fan of halfback Hugh McElhenny as I was, this game would further cement a place for him in my heart as the greatest 49er, EVER!

He found the end zone three times all within a 10-minute span of the first quarter. First he hauled in a 51-yard reception from Tittle. On the team's second possession, he sprinted 39 yards and scored again, and following the conversion, the 49ers led 14-0. Once again, he broke loose and found the end zone 39 yards later, giving the 49ers a 21-0 lead.

His third trip to the end zone followed a fumble by Ollie Matson, and this time he scampered 25 yards for another touchdown. The PAT was again successful, and the 49ers held a 28-0 lead as the quarter ended. Eighteen of the points came from my favorite player, McElhenny.

But the scoring outburst was far from being completed. After the ensuing kickoff, the 49ers drove 66 yards to a score that was set up following a pass interception by defensive back Jimmy Cason. Tittle's second scoring drive put the 49ers up 35-0, as Floyd Sagely scored on the one-yard toss.

Fort Ord finally got on the scoreboard with just 25 seconds to go in the first half. Matson, who was having a tough day in general, dashed 13 yards to the one-inch line. From there, Dave Mann followed with a line-plunge to end the first half, scoring with the 49ers in front, 35-7.

The 49ers scored again in the third quarter with Cason throwing a 15-yard pass to Floyd Sagely, his second receiving touchdown of the day that mounted the score to 42-7.

Fort Ord closed out the scoring late in the third quarter as 49ers' quarterback, Jimmy Powers, desperation pass was tipped by two Warriors, with end Gene Mitcham lateraling the ball to Dave Mann, who sprinted 46 yards for the touchdown.

The final score was the 49ers 42, Fort Ord 14.

"Our team did not feel those soldiers were pampered in any way. They played their hearts out and were very competitive throughout the game," said Buck Shaw. With that said, Fort Ord head coach Bill Abbey compared the 49ers to the Rams: "The 49ers first team is far superior, but the Rams have much better depth."

27

Jinx? What Jinx?

The afternoon of October 9, 1952, rookie halfback Hugh McElhenny played one of his best NFL games ever—one in which 49ers' fans will never forget. Team owner Tony Morabito had special reason not to forget it, and that reason had little to do with McElhenny.

It dated back to his earliest dealings with owner/head coach George "Papa Bear" Halas of the Chicago Bears. Halas was one of many NFL owners who had discouraged Morabito from even thinking about fielding a pro football team way back in the early 1940s. Although Halas later had voted in favor of a San Francisco franchise, somehow it backfired.

When the AAFC was born, the 49ers spent four glorious years in debtor's prison. Finally, in 1950 they made it to the NFL, or so Morabito thought. George Preston Marshall of the Washington Redskins charitably told Morabito:

"You still haven't seen the day. You're not a member of the NFL until you beat the Bears," (better known as the "Monsters of the Midway" for their bruising style of play). Morabito was stung.

The 49ers played the Bears twice in 1950, losing both games, 32-20 and 17-0. A season later, the team from the "Windy City" would claim a pair of victories: 24-7 and 13-7. That made four straight losses to Halas.

All of this would lead up to the 1952 encounter with the Bears as the stigma of losing to Chicago was eating away at Morabito. Were the Bears a jinx? The 49ers' owner uttered to Coach Shaw: "I no longer want to beat the Bears; I want to kill them!"

It was a very dreary day at Wrigley Field in Chicago, and things were about to change for the 49ers with Y. A. Tittle at the helm.

Right off the bat, it seemed that the outcome would be different for the City by the Bay. Tittle came out firing: first a 19-yard completion to Gordy Soltau, then another toss to McElhenny equaled the previous yardage, as the drive would reach the Bears' one-yard line. From there, Joe Perry plunged into the end zone giving San Francisco an early 7-0 lead.

The Bears knew one touchdown did not win a game. The sellout crowd of 48,000 at Wrigley Field bellowed in glee after Tittle was trapped in the end zone for a safety. The score now read 49ers 7, Bears 2.

Now the 49ers' defense got involved. Hardy Brown's pass deflection went into the hands of his teammate, Leon Wagner, who returned the interception 20 yards to the Bears' 39-yard line. From there, McElhenny and Perry took over. The former's 25-yard burst gave the 49ers a first and goal at the five, before Perry's second touchdown and subsequent conversion increased the team's margin to 12 (14-2) as the first quarter ended.

The Bears would bounce back as quarterback Bob Williams hit Bill Schroeder on a 56-yard pass play setting up a first down at the 49ers' eight-yard line. The Bears' Fred Morrison's eight-yard scoring run cut the margin to 14-9.

The 49ers' defensive unit stalled any Chicago attempt to get back into the game.

In the second quarter, McElhenny fielded a Bears' punt at his own six-yard line and dazzled the crowd by returning the punt 94 yards for a touchdown and into the record books.

Surprisingly, no blocks were thrown by the 49ers on the punt return, as he ran straight up the center of the field, making a 90-degree left turn on his own 23-yard line, and raced to the sideline. Two Chicago ends thought they had him trapped and closed in on the elusive 49er, but McElhenny made another 90-degree turn and headed for pay dirt—leaving the rest of the Bears in his cloud of dust, while his teammates simply stood there nodding to one another in admiration.

The return also was an amazement to Halas. Never one to mince his words, Halas said, "That was the damnedest run I've ever seen in football!"

Later McElhenny was to say casually, "I didn't think it was that long a run. If I'd known I was starting on my own six, I would have let the ball roll into the end zone."

At the halftime break, the 49ers carried a 21-9 advantage into the locker room, and they were beginning to sniff their first victory against the Bears. Remember, the 49ers did not have in mind to simply beat the Bears; they wanted to destroy them!

In the second half, Albert took over for Tittle, who had wrenched his back. Almost immediately, he marched the team 46 yards for another score to increase the 49ers' lead to 28-9. Soltau added a 39-yard field goal, as the 49ers took an insurmountable 31-9 lead after three quarters.

A pass interception led to the final Bears' touchdown in the fourth quarter, but the 49ers were not done scoring. Defensive ends

Ed Henke and Bob Momsen corralled Bears' quarterback in his own end zone for a safety. The 49er offense added another score as Bobby White capped a 71-yard drive with a four-yard run off left tackle.

Just before the final gun, the 49ers got a little playful in the play-calling, as tackle Leo Nomellini lined up in the backfield. Albert gave him the ball for one play. (His only other claim to fame as a ball carrier was against the Fort Ord Warriors during the preseason).

The big ole tackle's lone carry would pick up five yards, but not before he fumbled. In the official stats, he was credited with a five-yard run and a fumble lost.

Final score: 49ers 40, Bears 16!

The jinx of the Bears' supremacy was over. The score itself was something to treasure. The Chicago fans showed their appreciation to McElhenny by giving him a standing ovation when he left the field.

Halas had one other reaction about his performance: "This guy is unfair. The commissioner should make him play with a different team every week."

Former Bears' quarterback, Johnny Lujack, chimed in and said, "He's one of the best running backs I've seen in a long, long time."

After the game, McElhenny was about to receive his coronation into "royalty" as teammate Albert bestowed the crown upon him saying, "You're now the King," as he awarded the game ball to McElhenny for his part in the triumph.

On the day, McElhenny averaged 40.3 yards on three punt returns, 12 carries for 114 yards, four receptions and scored two touchdowns as three other scores were nullified by penalties. Perry added two more touchdowns, and Soltau gathered in more than 100 yards receiving in the game and would add a field goal in the impressive victory.

Owner Tony Morabito.

Kezar Stadium.

Kezar clock.

Jim Lawson, Lawrence "Buck" Shaw, and Phil Bengston.

Opening day at St. Mary's training camp.

Frankie Albert.

Schabarum, Perry, McElhenny and Tittle.

Tittle on a bootleg.

Joe Perry.

McElhenny congrats Perry for reaching 1,000 yards rushing in 1953.

Hugh McElhenny.

McElhenny hurdles for short gain in Pro Bowl.

McElhenny on a sweep against the Packers.

1955 49ers offense.

John Henry Johnson.

Y. A. Tittle.

McElhenny, Perry, Tittle, and Johnson
form the "Million Dollar Backfield."

Clay Matthews makes tackle against the Rams.

McElhenny, Perry, and Leo Nomellini get their jerseys retired by 49ers.

Albert, Perry, Tittle and McElhenny.

John Brodie.

Brodie to McElhenny to Beat Colts in 1957.

Joe Arenas.

Smith scores a touchdown against the Bears.

Jimmy Cason and Gordy Soltau.

Wilson hauls in completion against the Lions.

Billy Wilson Day in 1957.

Owens catches "alley-oop" to beat Detroit in 1957.

Clyde Connor receives Hawaiian greeting.

Connor makes reception against the Steelers.

Leo Nomellini.

St. Clair blocks attempted field goal.

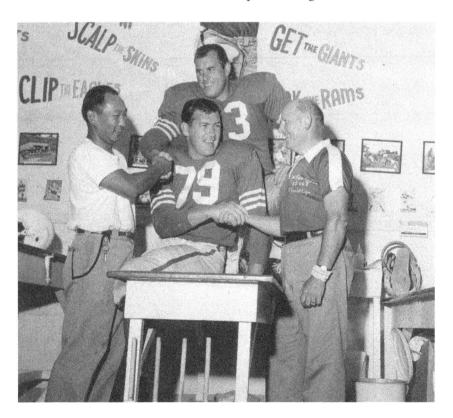

St. Clair offers his hand to trainer Schmidt.

Charlie Powell.

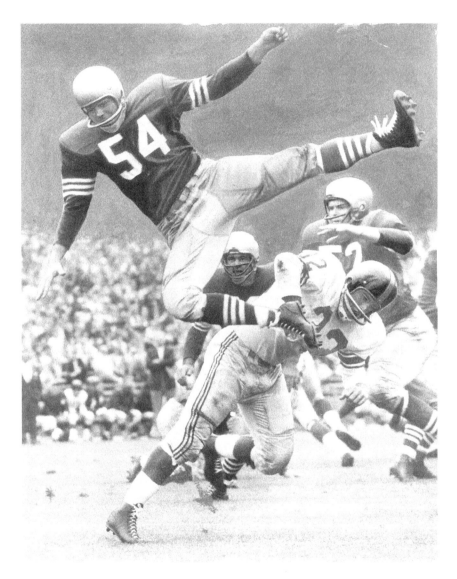

Marv Matuzak goes airborne to block punt.

Bruno Banducci and Head Coach Frankie Albert.

Hardy Brown.

Matt Hazeltine.

Dickey Moegle picks up yardage.

Abe Woodson.

John Strzkalski.

Dave Baker breaks up a pass.

49ers in Roller Derby action at Kezar Pavilion.
(Photo courtesy of Jim Fitzpatrick)

Coach Burnett with 49ers basketball players: Henke, McElhenny, St. Clair, Wilson, Soltau and Owens.

R. C. Owens.

49ers Majorette Deanna Cope.

Jan Jeffers with 49ers mascot Clementine.

49ers entertainment director Robert Olmstead.

Hopalong Cassidy at Kezar.

Author Martin Jacobs with Joe Perry.

28

A Win With "Lady Luck"

Call it divine intervention. It was unbelievable! Quarterback Y. A. Tittle and fullback Joe Perry took full advantage of a miscue— a fumble—as it aided San Francisco's comeback win, in a crucial Western Division game.

GAME SETTING: Detroit's Briggs Stadium, October 16, 1955, in front of 51,438 rained-soaked fans from a hailstorm. The conditions on the field were far less than favorable—for any team—let alone for a miraculous comeback victory for the visitors from California.

The two-minute warning had just been issued as the clock's hands slowly circled the dial, and when it displayed 0:00 ending the game, the Lions would be victorious. But it was not to be. The 49ers had trailed by 18 points (24-6) at that time.

So how did San Francisco's rally come about? Was it a eureka moment like when gold was discovered? A Disneyland fairytale? Divine intervention? Luck? Talent?

Let's take a look at what took place throughout the game that would set the stage and play into the win.

In the first quarter, Detroit capitalized on halfback Dickey Moegle's fumble on the opening kickoff and took a quick 7-0 lead.

John Henry Johnson added three more fumbles in the slush during the first quarter and now Joe Perry would become the go-to guy.

Despite falling behind 21-0 so quickly, San Francisco refused to quit.

The Lions built up an insurmountable 24-6 fourth-quarter advantage, before rookie halfback Moegle swept into the end zone on a 10-yard run cutting the lead margin to 24-13. Moegle's scamper and the subsequent defensive stand seemed to have ignited the 49ers... and the rally had begun!

The following series, 49ers' defensive back Rex Berry picked off a Lions' Harry Gilmer pass, returning the errant throw 44 yards for another 49ers' score. Following the conversion, the 49ers were down by four, 24-20.

The winning drive was behind the weatherproof arm of Tittle. The 49ers drove 57 yards as both Hugh McElhenny and Billy Wilson were on the receiving end of Tittle's tosses, while the churning legs of Perry and Moegle put the team in position to win the game with 1:50 left on the scoreboard clock.

Tittle described how the winning play came about. "On fourth down, I called a play," said Tittle, "that sent Joe Arenas faking into the line, as I would leap a jump pass to Soltau, cutting into the left corner of the end zone. Perry was the trailer just in case trouble developed.

But, I fumbled the handoff and Perry saw me drop the ball, as he didn't follow Soltau. Perry ran to my left hollering for me to pitch him the ball! I grabbed it and did what he said. He picked it up and ran around the corner past diving defenders to get our winning score. That was all there was to it."

The game was played in a rainstorm, but it didn't affect Tittle's passing game. He would complete 15 of his 31 tosses for 315 yards.

Assistant coach Frankie Albert stated, "That was the greatest exhibition of throwing a wet ball I have ever seen."

Moegle, a 20-year-old rookie from Rice, nicknamed the "Baby Face Assassin," returned three kickoffs for 139 total yards and did a yeoman's work on defense knocking down six passes. He also picked up crucial yards in the pivotal fourth-quarter comeback as he filled in for the ailing McElhenny.

The 49ers, who were usually quiet after a game, were a happy back-pounding group following the big win. McElhenny gave a rousing locker room speech and suggested the game ball be given to the "Colonel" Tittle. Co-captain and defensive end Clay Matthews agreed.

An exuberant 49ers' head coach Red Strader told the team following the win, "What I liked most of all, you boys didn't lose your poise even when you were down 18 points. You were just tremendous in the clutch. Lord knows, we had plenty of bad breaks and it was an uphill fight. We showed real caliber playing above our misfortunes. I'm certainly proud of this group."

29

A Game They Love to Hate

During the 1950s, these two rivals, the 49ers and Los Angeles Rams, went at each other for ten glorious years, playing in front of close to two million spectators—a figure unmatched in today's sports for an equal number of contests.

Rivals that started once San Francisco entered the NFL (in 1950), these two teams would meet a total of 28 times during the Golden Age.

The Rams held a 17-10-1 advantage during this period, but this was a rivalry that had more to do with emotion than numbers. It was geographic in nature: Northern California vs. Southern California, with two teams from the same division.

"We always hated those Ram horns," said receiver R. C. Owens. "In the 1950s, the Rams were kind of like All-Stars. You know, they had Mr. Everything at every position. Beating the Rams was it. Every game we played them, we fought, we scratched. Hell, Les Richter (Ram linebacker) once bit me! Ask Y. A. Tittle, Bob St. Clair, or Hugh McElhenny about the week leading up to the games. There was fire in the water, they would say."

The Rams and 49ers have produced a wealth of unforgettable moments, which were seen in the fog-swept Kezar and the sunny Los Angeles Memorial Coliseum. The Rams had a team loaded with talent, despite the retirement of legendary quarterback Bob Waterfield at the conclusion of the 1952 season.

They were prohibitive favorites coming into the 1953 season. They were league champions in 1951. Norm "The Flying Dutchman" Van Brocklin was now the lone quarterback to lead his team that was loaded with stars and included players who formed the "Bull Elephant" backfield—Dan Towler, Tank Younger, Skeet Quinlan, and Vitamin Smith—in all its awesome power. In addition, the Rams had the two best receivers in the league in Elroy "Crazy Legs" Hirsch and Tom Fears.

The Rams played at Kezar on October 4, 1953, in a game that was loaded with not only talent but 10 future Hall of Famers as well. Five Rams: quarterback Van Brocklin, defensive back Dick "Night Train" Lane, ends Elroy Hirsch and Fears, and defensive end Andy Robustelli. They would take on the 49ers' five future enshrinees: Tittle, Perry, McElhenny, Nomellini and St. Clair.

The 49ers were in their eighth year of existence and only their third year in the NFL. They were regarded as upstarts to NFL competition, as they finished the 1952 campaign at 7-5-0.

Prior to the matchup of California teams, San Francisco had opened the season defeating Philadelphia 31-21, which was marred by a 15-minute free swinging brawl that broke out during the game. The fight was considered a draw, but the momentum seemed to light a fire under the 49ers, as they prepared to host the Rams. Of all of the games the 49ers and Rams played over the years, the one played that day was one of the most memorable ones in the eyes of the fans—including this book's author.

October 4, 1953

Rams	10	10	7	3	30
49ers	0	7	14	10	31

With just six minutes into the first quarter, the expected aerial duel between Van Brocklin and Tittle was under way as the Rams drew first blood.

In the huddle, Van Brocklin would call one of his favorite plays "Seabiscuit."

The players broke the huddle following Van Brocklin's call: "Seabiscuit" to the post...everyone block...on two!" (Bob Boyd, another Ram swift end, was dubbed "Seabiscuit" on this particular play by his field general, as the play worked as it was drawn up).

Boyd hauled in the 66-yard spiral from his quarterback, as he beat 49ers' Rex Berry on the play. The kick by Ben Agajanian was good to lead, 7-0.

The Rams increased their margin to 10-0, when Tittle's pass was intercepted by Lane, which would lead to Agajanian's 22-yard field goal. The second quarter not only mirrored the total on the scoreboard, but fans would also see another seven-yard scoring strike from Van Brocklin to Hirsch and a 37-yard kick by Agajanian, which doubled the visitor's tally.

The hometown crowd of over 40,000 would be steamed and vengeful as never been seen before. As a result, fans sporadically threw beer bottles and cushions down onto the playing field. However, it did serve as a wake-up call for the 49ers.

With a 20-0 lead, the Rams had the ball on its own 13-yard line when they decided to run a trick play that failed, as Van Brocklin's perfectly thrown pass to Lane was dropped.

Rams' head coach Pool later said that the play had been planned in advance.

The 49ers, given new life by the foiled trick play, would put their first points on the scoreboard when Tittle's eight-yard pass to Billy Wilson cut the Rams' margin to 20-7 at the break.

Following the second-half kickoff, the 49ers struck quickly as Tittle tossed the ball to McElhenny, who lateraled to Joe Perry, who scampered into the end zone, capping a 14-play (12 rushing plays) 68 yards, cutting the Rams' lead to 20-14.

McElhenny ran the play perfectly, as seven of the Rams' defenders followed the reigning 1952 NFL Rookie of the Year, even after he lateraled to the "Jet"—who carried the other four players into the end zone. Perry then offered the ball to one of the visitors as a memento.

Following the ensuing kickoff, the Rams refused to quit. They mixed in several runs by Towler and Younger and short passes by Van Brocklin to eat up 90 yards of Kezar's grass in 11 plays, capped off by Younger's one-yard plunge. This increased the visitors' margin to 27-14.

The 49ers' defense got in on the scoring plays. Defensive back Leon Wagner recovered a Van Brocklin fumble at the Rams' 20-yard stripe. From there, the ball was advanced nine yards, then from the 11 when Perry got the call. He would follow his blockers up the middle on a trap play, cutting the margin to 27-21 as the third quarter came to an end.

The 49ers had momentum heading into the final quarter of action. Rex Berry intercepted a Van Brocklin pass at the Rams' 48, returning the errant toss to the 30-yard line. Tittle then engineered a seven-play drive, setting up Billy Mixon's (the heralded rookie out of Georgia) first professional touchdown. His four-yard burst tied up the score.

Gordy Soltau's kick gave the home team its first lead at 28-27. To say that the 49er fans at Kezar were in a frenzy would be an understatement.

But the Rams refused to do an el foldo. With less than four minutes left in the quarter, their drive reached the San Francisco 11, where on fourth and inches, the field goal unit was sent out onto the field. Agajanian's kick at the three-minute mark put the Rams back in front, 30-28.

The play looked like it would have clinched a Rams' victory, but hold on—with 1:40 left in the game, San Francisco's defense held the Rams to a three-and-out, forcing a punting situation. McElhenny fielded a Van Brocklin punt at the 49ers' seven-yard line, and "swivel-hipped" his way 93 yards for the apparent go-ahead touchdown, but it was called back due to a clipping penalty by St. Clair.

Ordinarily, one denies such a penalty and stoutly defends the teammate accused of it, but McElhenny had a different philosophy: "Of course he clipped the guy," he said, "Do you think I could have scored if he didn't? He got called for it; that's it. It's a chance you take."

Following the penalty, the 49ers had to start deep in their own territory. Tittle called a sideline pass to stop the clock. The Rams' defense was deployed against a deep pass, and as such, Tittle called an audible at the line of scrimmage. The new play was a screen pass to McElhenny.

The "King" followed Nomellini and Banducci, who would make tremendous blocks to spring their teammate for a 71-yard gain, before the Rams' Woodley Lewis nudged McElhenny out of bounds at the nine-yard line. That play really zapped "The King." "I was tired," he later confessed. "If I'd been fresh," he said, "I don't think he could have touched me."

San Francisco rallied with less than 1:15 on the clock. Runs by Perry and Mixon only gained three yards as time was running out.

Fifty-one seconds were all that separated the home team from victory or defeat. Tittle ran a bootleg to the right and was hauled down at the Rams' five-yard line. However, in his zeal, he had failed to get the ball in front of the goal post for Soltau's field-goal attempt from the right hash mark.

The scoreboard clock revealed just 0:36 remaining, as Soltau came in to attempt the winning kick—in one of the wildest endings anyone had ever seen, in what appeared to be a miscommunication between Soltau and Tittle, as the team was in the huddle for full a 31 seconds.

As a result, the 49ers were flagged for a delay of game, pushing the distance back five yards to the 10-yard stripe, but the angle was reduced. This strategy by Tittle came as a revelation to Buck Shaw. He later confessed he almost had a heart attack after he had sent in Soltau to try a field goal in the final 30 seconds.

"Tittle took so long in the huddle, I thought we'd never get the kick away before the final gun." Shaw said.

"I never lost track of time," Tittle said after the game. "I was ticking off the seconds in my head. I did not want the Rams to have any time left for a comeback." No matter. As it worked out, five seconds still remained when Soltau made the kick. The 49ers won the battle, 31-30.

Phil Bengtson, the 49ers' line coach, called it "the greatest game I ever saw, either as a player or coach."

The 49ers' players won it, though Shaw was emotionally drained. "The extra practice sessions during the week sharpened our defense against a strong Rams' passing attack. It paid off," he said.

Van Brocklin was limited to 20 completions out of 34 passes and a mere 272 yards. From those figures, one can speculate what the 49ers' pass defense was like before Shaw ordered the extra workouts.

And on the losing side, Rams' head coach Hampton Pool wasn't convinced his team lost, but they did. Pool was so impressed. "McElhenny?" he said. "I've never seen anything quite like him. I had warned my players about him in advance that they could not let up on him."

When it was over, it was the 49ers who shocked the Rams in a typical "cliff-hangar" style that autumn, Sunday afternoon, as the field-goal kickers were the decisive factors. This game between these California rivals was just one of many thrilling games played between them during the Golden Age.

Some of the other memorable games included:

November 9, 1954: Rams 42, 49ers 34. The Rams and 49ers pile up a combined 868 total yards in this high-scoring contest.

October 7, 1956: 49ers 33, Rams 30. Five Rams' fumbles and Gordy Soltau's four field goals led to the upset victory.

October 6, 1957: 49ers 23, Rams 20. R. C. Owens' "alley-oop" pass play from Y. A. Tittle with 3:15 left in game beat the Rams.

November 10, 1957: Rams 37, 49ers 24. A record 102,368 at the Los Angeles Memorial Coliseum watched the offensive fireworks.

30

Joe Perry Day

On August 28, 1955, before the delight of 41,604 fans, fullback Joe "The Jet" Perry made his day a memorable one. His fans had been demanding for several years to honor Perry, and finally he received it.

Only one other 49er player had ever received a "day," and that was Norm Standlee in 1950.

(Author's note: It was Standlee whom Perry replaced as starting offensive fullback when he came to the 49ers in 1948. Perry was only 20 years of age at that time, as he had just completed two years of service with the U.S. Navy.)

Adding a little frosting to the cake, he was named team captain by coach Buck Shaw before they played the Cleveland Browns after the ceremony at Kezar.

Like Jesse Owens and Joe Louis, Perry brought a high skill and dignity to the 49ers. NFL opponents had come to accept him as an able, sportsmanlike performer, with all the moves of a graceful tiger.

His walk was that of a champion, possessed with talent of aggression; only he used it to make a living. Every inch a gentlemen and sportsman, Perry always had been a credit to his race and the game of football. His "day" was an appropriate honor.

"Perry is the only 49er, other than Y. A. Tittle, who knows every players' assignment on any given play," said head coach Buck Shaw modestly. "While watching game film, often Joe would pick out something not even the coaches had noticed."

The first time Perry ever carried the ball as a pro in 1946, he dashed 57 yards to a touchdown against the Buffalo Bills. And as a result, he would not stop running until he broke the NFL's all-time leading ground-gainer's rushing record during the 1958 season (surpassing Philadelphia's Steve Van Buren in the process).

On this day though, Perry ranked third in the NFL's all-time rushing stats with 4,116 yards behind Van Buren and Tony Canadeo of Green Bay.

(Author's note: The NFL failed to count Perry's two seasons that he played in the AAFC, 1948-49. If they had done so, Perry would hold the standard, with a 5.3 yards per carry that had not been surpassed.)

For the record, Perry was the only player in the NFL history, at that time, to gain 1,000 yards rushing in two consecutive seasons (1953-54).

During pregame ceremonies, the "Jet" was bestowed many gifts by civic dignitaries, from both San Francisco and Oakland, Norm Standlee, the Gold Rushers, former teammates and the fans. Jerry Lynch served as the Master of Ceremony and Chairman of the "Joe Perry Day" committee.

His gifts included a 21-inch RCA Victor color TV set from his teammates; a General Electric "Kitchen," from head coach Red Strader and his staff; a master bedroom suite from W. & J. Sloan Company; a living room suite from the 49ers' management; a 16-millimeter motion picture projector, plus prints of the 1953 and 1954 Hi-Lite films, from Burgermeister brewing company; and an Ampex 600 tape recorder from station KLX radio station (Perry's off-season employer).

Among Perry's other gifts were a set of golf clubs, a bowling ball, a collection of jazz and classical records to be considered for his radio show where he worked as disc jockey and sports commentator (cum laude) "with honors."

Perry humbly acknowledged the truckload of gifts with his heartfelt appreciation to his mother, his family, friends, teammates, team owners, coaches and his fans.

On his special day against the Browns, the hard-hitting, Mr. Outside-Inside Perry, all in one, carried the ball brilliantly, continuing his mastery over the 1954 NFL Champions, picking up 116 yards on 20 carries (a 5.8 average) with his longest run of the day—33 yards, following a key block by 49er rookie halfback, Carroll Hardy, in leading San Francisco to a 17-14 exhibition game victory.

"Perry not only turned in a remarkable rushing job against a tough Browns' line, he was more determined today to put on a good show," said Buck Shaw. "Joe is an inspiration to everyone on the team. Each time Perry came off the field, he was full of emotion, all out to win."

His yardage in this game exceeded the total racked up on the ground by 44 by the entire Browns' cast. The Browns lost out only by the margin of a nine-yard field goal by Gordy Soltau (the only score in the first half), but the Browns were clearly outplayed by the 49ers, who parlayed a rock-ribbed defense, to Perry's depredations afoot, in fashioning their finest effort of the young season.

Browns' head coach, Paul Brown, packaged the 49ers victory in a few statements: "This was Joe Perry's day in more ways than one. For 2 ½ hours today, he gave us fits, and he was the difference. He'd be called to run inside tackle, get stopped, and squirt around end for six or seven yards. Those were crucial yards. They gave his team ball control and game control."

31

"Alley-Oop"

R. C. Owens was a 49ers' flanker during the Golden Age, whose impressive leaping ability earned him the nickname, "Alley-Oop." He was probably the most celebrated player in 49ers' team history. At six foot three, 210 pounds, he was a college basketball star at the College of Idaho.

During his senior season (1954-55) on the court, he put up some outstanding statistics. He would average 20 points a game while pulling down 19.8 rebounds. He and Elgin Baylor (the LA Lakers Hall of Famer) were basketball teammates. Baylor, a starting forward, wanted to go in the same direction as Owens and pursue the NFL, but he chose to stay with basketball and ended up playing 14 seasons in the NBA.

After college, Owens continued his basketball career and signed on with one of the best A.A.U. basketball championship teams in the country, the Buchan Bakers in Seattle. They toured Europe and played against Olympic teams from France, Italy, Spain, Canada, Poland and Czechoslovakia. They were the first American team to play behind the Iron Curtin since World War II.

Though Owens loved basketball, it was with football where Owens made his mark professionally. Because of his work ethic he earned the nickname "Overdrive," and was named to the Little All-America Team as an end following the 1954 season, which saw him tied for the top receiver position in the nation, with 48 catches for 948 yards and seven touchdowns.

Owens was drafted by the 49ers in the 14th round—160th over-all—in the 1956 draft. The 49ers mainly drafted him because of his ball-handling and jumping skills. He did not report to the 49ers until the summer of 1957 because of his commitment to basketball.

When he arrived at the 49ers' training camp he was considered a long shot to make a team already loaded at receiver with Billy Wilson, Gordy Soltau, Clyde Conner and Hugh McElhenny, who were all in the mix.

Going into their 12th season (1957), the 49ers had yet to either make the playoffs or catch the imagination of the Bay Area or create periodic excitement for the fans. The arrival of Hugh McElhenny in 1952 gave the 49er faithful something to cheer about, but back-to-back losing seasons, in 1955 and 1956, relegated the team back to mediocrity.

Frankie Albert was starting his second season as head coach in 1957 with a club that was picked to finish near the bottom of the six-team Western Conference. Something had to be done to bring the fans into the stadium—but what?

Welcome in the "alley-oop."

It made its debut during a preseason game against the Giants on an overcast August afternoon at Kezar, with the game winding down and the 49ers holding a slim, 17-15 margin. Y. A. Tittle flung a high, looping desperation pass towards the end zone. Owens leaped into the air, pulling in Tittle's toss for a touchdown.

"I was just trying to throw the ball away out of the end zone," quipped Tittle. "I just threw it away and he came down with it. It was just a lucky catch."

Not so, thought R. C. Owens. After the catch, he came up to Tittle on the sidelines and said, "I can catch that pass every time."

Offensive assistant coach Red Hickey figured they were on to something and called the play the "alley-oop." Before that play, nobody knew much about Owens except for his brief stint as a basketball player. He was not considered fast by receiver standards, but he could outjump any defensive back.

"When I was playing in college, receivers weren't jumping over defenders," Owens said. "I guess I was just blessed with my leaping ability."

No one really took the "alley-oop" seriously, but Tittle and Owens were having so much fun with it. Though, it would be a couple of more weeks before their accidental connection would be defined and put into the 49ers' playbook. The seeds for the "alley-oop" had been planted. The play became very popular with the fans and sportswriters who spent much of their game stories describing the unusual pass play.

Three weeks later against the Cardinals in Seattle, Owens snagged three passes for 109 yards and a touchdown to cement a spot on the roster. He also foreshadowed his trademark "alley-oop," along with another leaping catch—outjumping two defenders—in the 49ers' 27-21 victory.

"I guess you could say the 'alley-oop' was the same as the 'Hail Mary' pass you see today, except we didn't pray," Owens gushed.

Tittle and Owens worked on it in practice until the play was refined. Then the coaches put their heads together and devised ways to incorporate the element of surprise into the game plan with the "alley-oop."

Because of Owens' exceptional jumping ability, the concept was simple. As they designed it, Owens would flank right or left. At the snap, he would run deep downfield and curl back. None of the defensive backs could break through him without risking an interference call.

Execution in the distances of 40 to 50 yards, of course, could never be automatic. But the "alley-oop" upped the odds considerably in favor of the pass. Owens told Tittle not to throw a perfect spiral when he delivered the "alley-oop," but to put a little wobble on it. Tittle would throw the ball as high and as far as he could, while Owens would jog down the field, wait for the ball about 14-feet high and then outjump everyone around him.

"I always felt a wobbly pass gave me a chance to catch the front end or the back end of the football," said Owens. "In fact, the only difficult part of the play was the signals. In Tittle's terminology, left end was port, right end was rip and the tight end was X or Y, depending on which side of the line I was positioned.

"So my call for the 'alley-oop' in the huddle would go as example…'51 (pass pattern)…Y right…rip…alley-oop!' On that play I was the right end rip. Sometimes in the huddle, Tittle would just say, 'alley-oop on two.'"

During the 1957 season, the Tittle-Owens "alley-oop" combination worked five times for game-winning scores, with three coming in the last minute of games. The media also had their own name for the new play, calling it a "cliff-hanger."

Owens ended up playing five seasons with the 49ers from 1957-61. He had 176 receptions for 2,923 yards and 20 touchdowns. He also ran for a score. He also was also the first 1,000-yard receiver in team history, with his single-season best marks coming in 1961. That season, he caught 55 balls covering 1,032 yards (for an 18.8 yards per catch) and five touchdowns.

Following the 1961 season, Owens left the 49ers and signed with the Colts as a free agent. This was the first time an NFL player would leave one team and sign with a different team, thus creating the "Rozelle Rule," whereby the Commissioner would decide on compensation for the losing team. (Hence, Owens was directly responsible for the Rozelle Rule).

The 49ers failed to receive any compensation following Owens' departure because of the leagues "ex-post facto" rule at the time.

32

Albert at the Helm

I was not too surprised when Tony Morabito made his decision to pick Frankie Albert to take over the head coaching reins left behind by Red Strader, who was let go after a dismal 1955 season (4-8-0). He always had admiration for Albert, although his coaching experience was limited to just a couple of spring practices at Stanford, plus a brief association with Strader as a clerk filing information sent in by 49er talent scouts.

If rooting for Albert was all he needed, he would have been a success as a head coach. But it proved to be not enough. There was no doubt about one aspect. As a player, Albert gave more people more thrills over a longer period of time than any 49ers' player.

What the new coach had accomplished as a player drove the opposition mad, with his ingenious analytical brain and daring maneuvers as a quarterback—and a mighty little one at that. Perhaps as a head coach holding all the strings, he might do even better.

But this would not really work in his favor either; perhaps circumstances could. Although he arrived on the scene at a propitious time, he tried to restore the balance of power with a healthy 49ers' team.

Because of his lack of experience for head coaching, he had to lean heavily on his assistants for his vital transition to head coach. He rehired line coach Phil Bengston, end coach Red Hickey and chief scout Mark Duncan to join his staff.

At 36 years of age, Albert was the youngest coach in the NFL, but he was not the youngest ever to lead a team. That distinction belongs to Paul Brown of Cleveland, who was 34 when he first put together his invincible Browns in 1946.

With Albert's age, he could still be called a "boy wonder" IF his team produced a winning season. The great Knute Rockne was only 30 when he took over as head coach at Notre Dame.

Morabito pointed out in delineating the reasons for Albert's appointment: "As a player for seven years, Frankie did as much to establish the 49ers' popularity, as anyone. He was picked chiefly, because of his quality of leadership—and that is something so intangible, it cannot be defined. And he had it. We have observed him for 11 years and liked what we saw. Truthfully, he has been an inspiration. And not only to those with whom he played, but a lot of others.

"As for his experience, well...he was the original T-formation quarterback at Stanford for Clark Shaughnessy. He has been part of football for 17 years. Isn't that enough experience? We wouldn't for one minute think of throwing this young fellow to the wolves."

Said Gordy Soltau, "We wanted Albert because he's competent, and we'll do a job for him. He'll be able to rally the players better than anyone. We have all the confidence in him and we'll put him over. He's going to surprise a lot of people."

Albert was reminded that once he said he never wanted to be a head coach. He answered in typical style: "You can't plan too far ahead. The heart has to lead you. And I have always been unpredictable—just a left hander. It is what I know and love best. Whatever I have in the back of my mind for the future can wait, I hope, forever."

Albert got the deal he wanted worth $25,000 a year, with severance pay for the third if he was not rehired.

At the request of Albert, the 49ers would change the color of the helmet from scarlet to solid white—a throwback from the 1946 season—to begin his tenure as head coach in 1956.

The outlook for his first season as head coach, at best, seemed auspicious. The 49ers opened the season with a 33-30 win over the Rams, but success was short-lived, as this was the lone triumph in the first 7 games (1-6-0). Even in defeat, Albert had one theory and that he still operated the same way: hold onto the ball as this would keep the opposition from scoring. Going 4-0-1 over the last five games of the season was enough to keep Albert from being fired, as his team finished third in the Western Conference, with a 5-6-1 mark.

"All season long, our team was missing their assignments," Albert said, calling his team apathetic with a lackadaisical attitude. "Someday, sometime...when the moon is made of blue cheese...this team must learn, that in NFL competition, they have to play 60 minutes of all-out football or come up a loser."

Albert's second season fared better than his first as a result of winning five of the team's first six games and sitting atop the conference by mid-season. The 49ers would then lose three in a row on the road, falling to a 5-4 record. However, a three-game winning streak closed out the season at 8-4, their best mark since 1953.

The 49ers and the Lions ended up tied for the top spot in the Western Conference. Because of the tie, the teams would meet in the first NFL playoff game at Kezar, with the winner taking on the Cleveland Browns for the league championship. But that game ended in another agonizing loss when the Lions rallied from a 27-7 deficit to beat the 49ers, 31-27.

"I still can't believe that game," Albert said. "We were ahead and started playing conservative. That's what killed us. They scored once, then they scored twice, and the next thing you know, they were ahead. It was embarrassing. It just goes to show you how quickly things can happen on a football field."

Albert's final season would be bittersweet. During 49ers' practices, Albert could be seen sitting in his little golfer's portable chair, which was always beside the coach, and he seldom walked the sidelines.

At the beginning of the 1958 season, he was still a cocky boyish-looking "boy wonder." Three months later, there were streaks of gray in his dark brown hair, pouches of worry under his eyes, and lines in his face. When he saw the change in a mirror, he decided to give his resignation to Morabito at mid-season.

Morabito told Albert, "Think it over carefully, Frank," cautioned Vic. "There are still five games to go." There was no need to discuss contract technicalities. Frank's "contract," with both Tony and Vic was a handshake.

Football had always been fun and frolic to Albert when he was a player. His carefree attitude carried over into the deadly serious business of coaching. Undoubtedly, it was a prime factor in the comeback of 1956 and the highly successful campaign in 1957.

But Albert, like most extroverts, had an extremely sensitive side. His pride was crushed when the Rams humbled the 49ers 33-3 in the second game of the season, and his world practically fell apart when his team took a horrible 56-7 beating in Los Angeles.

"Honest to Knute Rockne," he told Emerson "Bud" Spencer, sports editor of the San Francisco News. "You'd think this team, who almost had a division title—and possibly a NFL championship—in their hands not so many months ago, would remember the priceless facts of football: never let down, or the cat you drowned will get up and scratch you."

Albert had always been a fighter, but there was no way to endure the pain he experienced as a head coach. He would be criticized during the season for the way he handled his two quarterbacks, Tittle and Brodie, whom he played musical chairs with.

He started Brodie in a game and jerked him out for Tittle and then rushed him in again. Albert was torn between which one to play. In truth, the Tittle-Brodie controversy was a huge distraction to the team and Albert knew it.

During a four-game road-trip, the 49ers only won one game and finished strong with a 6-6 record for fourth place in the Western Division. Two games aided to the strong finish, as the Packers were handled at home 48-21, and then just before Albert's decision to resign was made public, the 49ers ended the season on a high note: a 21-12 upset of the Colts.

In retrospect, Albert was under terrific strain from the moment he accepted the job, but he never did show his feelings much, considering the circumstances. That frustration was offset by the camaraderie and friendships Albert had established as one of the original 49ers.

"I liked certain aspects of coaching," he said impassively. "I enjoyed teaching the kids. I had good running backs to gamble with. You can't compare many backfields with McElhenny and Perry. Mac was the best open field runner from the 'T' that ever played. Perry was a different runner. He was good straight ahead, while Mac was always zigging and zagging around the field."

Albert added, "There were some real characters on those teams. St. Clair was one of them. He used to eat raw meat. We'd go to a nice restaurant, and he liked beef, so he'd order a steak or something.

He'd tell the waiter to just have the chef heat the meat. He didn't want it cooked, just warmed up. A few minutes later the chef would look out from the kitchen to see who was ordering their meat like that. He's one of the few guys from the old teams that could be playing today. He was that good and he had the size too. Besides Bob, Nomellini was a good one on the line. In his later years, he played only defense, but he was a pretty good offensive lineman, too."

Albert's final totals were 19 wins, 17 losses and a draw. Not bad for a "boy wonder" from Glendale, California.

33

A Wild Ride to the Finish

Not much was expected of Frankie Albert's 1957 team as he started in his second season as head coach. The 49ers were picked to finish near the bottom of the six-team Western Conference. But as usual, when predicting how the 49ers would finish, the sportswriters should have known better. In preseason games, the 49ers defeated the champion Giants, Redskins, Browns and Cardinals, losing only to the Rams. The consensus was that the 49ers had a good team but not a great team.

During the 1957 campaign, newspapers ran out of adjectives describing this exciting team. There were "cliff-hangers," "heartbreakers," last-second victories, and unbelievable plays that accounted for a winning 8-4 season, forcing a playoff game against the Lions.

In seven, of their eight regular season wins, the 49ers trailed in the second half. In six of those, they trailed in the fourth quarter. In five, they trailed in the last four minutes, and in four, they won in the last minute. Adding to the drama was the fatal heart attack suffered by owner Tony Morabito, the only owner the team had ever had, during a game at Kezar against the Chicago Bears.

The 49ers failed to win a championship in 1957, but there were some fabulous comebacks. Here's a recap, best described as a "roller coaster" season:

THE DEBUT OF THE "ALLEY-OOP" 49ers 23, Rams 20

In week 2, the heavily favored Los Angeles Rams met the 49ers at Kezar on October 6, before a sellout crowd of 59,000, as the teams took to the field. The faithful hopes were just for a respectable showing against the powerful Rams.

However, that thought died quickly as the Rams scored easily to take a 7-0 lead. Then in the second quarter, the 49er defense dug in. Surprisingly, they were handed a gift of two points, as the Rams' Tom Wilson was forced into the end zone by a bad pitchout and was tackled by Leo Nomellini. The safety seemed to be the spark that San Francisco needed.

With the 49ers driving towards downfield, Y. A. Tittle passed to Clyde Conner to the Ram 23-yard line, who then lateraled to Billy Wilson, who scored—giving the 49ers a 9-7 advantage.

Just before halftime, with 50 seconds left on the clock, Tittle dropped back to pass and aimed the ball for the corner of the end zone. In a spectacular motion, Owens leaped high and came down with the "alley-oop" pass for a touchdown, giving the home team a nine-point margin at 16-7.

After the break, as the Rams quickly got back into the game, as Norm Van Brocklin teamed up with Leon Clarke on a 70-yard pass play, cutting the 49ers' lead to 16-14. A pair of field goals would increase the margin to 20-14, with 11 minutes left in the game.

Unbelievable as it may seem, with just 3:15 remaining, Tittle and Owens pulled off another "alley-oop" pass play, and the 49ers upset the Rams. The 49ers were making believers out of all of us. They were the conquering heroes, knocking off the Rams.

TAMING THE "MONSTERS OF THE MIDWAY"
49ers 21, Bears 17

Week 3 saw the 49ers visit Chicago's Wrigley Field to face the Bears, which featured one of the NFL's most physical and strongest defenses.

Surprisingly, this game turned into a defensive struggle, as the first half ended scoreless, 0-0. The 49ers themselves were being blanked by a fierce Bears' defense.

In the third quarter, Chicago capitalized on a fumble by Hugh McElhenny on their own 33-yard line. Bears' fullback Rick Casares found the end zone with the game's first points. After falling behind by a touchdown, the 49er offense found their rhythm as well, as Tittle would connect on two passes to Billy Wilson and Owens, picking up 40 and 30 yards respectively to tie the score at 7-7.

San Francisco wasn't through scoring either. Late in the third quarter, the 49ers pulled off a surprise play. Tittle pitched out to half-back Joe Arenas, who faked a sweep and then passed 33 yards to end Clyde Conner, and the 49ers went ahead 14-7.

In the fourth quarter, the Bears went ahead 17-14 on a field goal with 4:29 left. Tittle, dueling the clock, drove the 49ers down-field with just 0:27 seconds left to play. Would the 49ers pull off another miracle?

As the ball was snapped, Owens was knocked down at the line of scrimmage at the Bears seven-yard line, but he crawled into the end zone on his hands and knees, just as Tittle threw the ball low and hard. Owens caught the ball for the winning touchdown.

"After that miraculous catch, I think if Owens had run for mayor of San Francisco, he'd have won," Albert said after the game. "A legend was in the making" (referring to Owens).

THIS ONE'S FOR TONY 49ers 21, Bears 17

The score in this week 5 contest was the same as the one in week 3, but the circumstances were very different.

October 27 was a cold and gloomy day. Fog had billowed in early from the Pacific, three miles to the west of Kezar, and hung like a pall over the capacity crowd of nearly 60,000 boisterous fans.

It wasn't the weather, however, that depressed the spirits of those crammed into the ancient bowl. Fans had watched in disbelief and despair as the 49ers dropped two touchdowns in the arrears to an aroused Bears' team in less than two minutes of play.

Then tragedy struck the 49ers just minutes into the second half, when Bears' quarterback Ed Brown tried a roll out around his own left end and was thrown for a five-yard loss by Bill Herchman. At that moment, 49er owner Tony Morabito collapsed from a heart attack while sitting in the guest box. The tragic announcement came to the 49er fans in the third quarter, and there was stunned silence.

The 49ers started the third quarter down,17-7, but the news of Morabito's passing gave them an emotional lift. The 49ers put on a fierce pass rush on quarterback Brown's attempted pass, which was picked off by Herchman, who ran 54 yards for a touchdown. Suddenly, the 49ers cut the Bears' lead to 17-14.

Then lightning struck the Bears again. This time, Marv Matuszak deflected another Brown pass, and Dickey Moegle grabbed it and returned it 40 yards to the Bears' 11-yard line. With just 12 minutes left to play, again Tittle pulled off his magic. He faded back to pass and found Wilson clear in the right flat for the winning touchdown. How could 49er football get any better?

The win was San Francisco's third come-from-behind victory of the season. But that news was secondary. "I'd rather have lost the game by 100 points than to lose Tony," said a saddened Albert.

The 49ers stood at 4-1 with the best record in the NFL. But for all the sorrow from the owner's passing and the 49er come-from-behind win, next Sunday would come, and so would Detroit.

NOTHING IS OVER UNTIL WE SAY IT IS
49ers 35, Lions 31

The week 6 game at Kezar vs. Detroit attracted the largest crowd of the season to date, 59, 702, on a bright sunny day. The 49ers had the NFL's best record at 4-1. They were coming off an emotionally charged win over Chicago following Morabito's passing.

In the game, the 49ers built up a commanding 28-7 lead, but late in the game, the Lions scored three touchdowns to burst ahead 31-28, with little time left on the clock.

By now, if one didn't believe in 49ers' comebacks, there would be no hope. With 1:28 left, the 49ers took possession on their own 22. On the winning drive, Tittle completed three of four passes that were hauled in by Wilson and McElhenny, placing the ball at the Lions' 41-yard line, as the clock was displaying its last 11 seconds of the game.

Tittle knew there was only one thing to do. Owens knew it, too. So did long-time 49ers' radio play-by-play announcer Bob Fouts, whose voice was often heard in those days on 49ers' highlight films, screaming before the ball was snapped, "This has got to be the "alley-oop! There's no time remaining."

Fouts called it perfectly, as Tittle rolled to his right. Then like a bird transfixed by a snake, he lofted a desperation "alley-oop" pass to Owens at the goal line. Owens timed his leap to perfection and came down with the ball between two Lions' defenders. Tittle and Owens had hooked up again. The 49ers had won!

"Fans collapsed everywhere," reported Bob Brachman of the *San Francisco Examiner*, "and immediately the siren on the stadium ambulance let go with a blast and headed in the direction of the press box. A fan had died, overcome by emotion. Hundreds of fans ran onto the field. Even the mounted policemen urged their horses through the milling mob to bring some kind of order from this hysteria."

The intersections around the stadium were solid humanity. Cars were backed up for blocks, horns blaring. Firecrackers went off, and on street corners, groups of revelers chanted "49ers!" and waved pennants. The win gave the 49ers a 5-1 record and a two-game lead in the Western Conference with six games remaining.

At the time, Tittle called it the greatest game of his career. He eclipsed Albert's team record by completing 21 of 28 passes in a game.

NEW YORK, NEW YORK! 49ers 27, Giants 17

By week 10, the battered and bruised 49ers were coming off a three-game losing streak, and Albert gave the 49ers the day off in New York before facing the Giants. This was a do-or-die game, with just three games left on the schedule.

The Giants were battling the Browns for first place in the Eastern Conference, while the 49ers were a 10-point underdog. Bob St. Clair was coming back from a shoulder injury, and the 49ers were feeling optimistic.

The day of the game, there was snow on the ground at Yankee Stadium, and the temperature was in the low 20s. This time it was the Giants who might have been overlooking the 49ers.

Y. A. Tittle, nursing a pulled leg muscle, led a revitalized 49ers' offense, as his "ball-hawking" defense forced six fumbles by the Giants. Tittle was superb, completing 11 of 16 passes and running five times for 49 vital yards. The 49ers played probably their best game of the season in beating the Giants. Suddenly, the 49ers were feeling pretty good again.

GIVE IT TO "THE KING" 49ers 17, Colts 13

Week 11 saw the 49ers tied with Baltimore and Detroit for first place in the Western Conference, with a record of 6-4 and just two games remaining. 49ers' fans knew the importance of the game.

The day before the game, 49ers fans, escorted by a police squad on horseback, lined up outside Kezar to buy the remaining 5,000 tickets that went on sale in the morning. The long lines rolled back into Golden Gate Park, while some 15,000 fans unable to get seats for the game poured out of the City and headed for Reno, Lake Tahoe—anywhere over the boundaries of the 150-mile TV blackout.

The game with the Colts lived up to the billing. Almost immediately on the 49ers' opening drive, the Colts were called for pass interference on McElhenny on the one-yard line, and the 49ers scored first. The Colts quickly tied it up, as Milt Davis picked off a Tittle pass and ran 75 yards for a score to lead 7-6. Nomellini blocked the conversion. In the second quarter, Soltau booted the 49ers further ahead, 10-6.

Still throughout the afternoon, the Colts often appeared to have a sounder team. Johnny Unitas, the Colts' remarkable quarterback, handled his team well, although he was under strong pressure from the 49ers' defensive line of Ed Henke, Bob Toneff, Matt Hazeltine, Marv Matusak, Bill Herchman and Karl Rubke most of the afternoon.

The Colts' quarterback worked carefully to set up the most spectacular touchdown of the game, an 82-yard scoring pass to halfback Lenny Moore. This put Baltimore in front 13-10, with four minutes and 36 seconds into the third quarter.

Halfback Hugh McElhenny, filling in for end Clyde Conner, aided the 49ers of much-needed speed at the end and flanker position. He had already caught seven passes for 153 yards that afternoon.

The score seesawed back and forth, as both defenses dominated the game until late in the fourth quarter.

With just under a minute left to play in the game, Tittle maneuvered the 49ers down into scoring position with a 43-yard pass play to McElhenny. But Tittle, who was 21 for 34 tosses, injured his hand on the play when the Colts' defense converged on him, causing a sudden muscle spasm in his injured leg. Two teammates assisted him off the field.

Called to arms under dramatic circumstances that no Hollywood scriptwriter could have dreamed up, Coach Albert had no choice but to send in the neophyte, inexperienced rookie quarterback John Brodie onto the field.

Brodie, who had played something less than 10 minutes through the 10 previous games, had the Western Conference title riding in his hands. He tried one pass from the 14-yard line that went astray.

With 0:47 seconds left on the clock, knowing a tie was useless to them in their quest for their first division championship, the 49ers huddled facing fourth down.

The rookie signal caller asked his teammates, "What the hell do we do now?" McElhenny spoke up. "Davis is playing me too loose. I can get away. Just throw it to the left corner of the end zone, and I'll be there," said McElhenny.

Under a heavy pass rush, McElhenny raced straight down at Colt rookie defensive back, Milt Davis, in the end zone and suddenly cut sharply to the sideline. The pass was perfect. McElhenny gathered in the pass for the winning touchdown.

"I just threw it (the ball) and prayed," Brodie would later admit.

Team captain Bob St. Clair awarded the game ball to McElhenny. "Usually we like to give the ball to a defensive player," St. Clair said in his presentation speech. "But today, Mac's the man."

"I'll split the ball with you," McElhenny hollered to Brodie. But Brodie declined. "I'm the luckiest son of a gun in the world," said Brodie. "But that ball belongs to you. I'd like to put my name on it, though."

Coach Albert then climbed on a bench to make another speech. "Fellows," he said, "don't forget we still have one more game." He didn't finish his speech.

"Two more, Coach!" St. Clair yelled, as the team roared.

All was not sweetness and light after the game. Web Ewbank, the Colts' coach, took the defeat bitterly. Ewbank claimed McElhenny pushed Davis in completing the touchdown pass, which gave the 49ers the game. "R. C. Owens used to push defenders to complete passes until the other clubs caught on," said Ewbank. "Now McElhenny has learned the trick."

Said McElhenny, in ambiguous rebuttal, "On the touchdown pass, I didn't touch him, and he didn't touch me."

As the 49ers' fans filed out of Kezar, hundreds of them lined up at ticket booths to buy the few remaining tickets for the following week's showdown with the Packers. Doubtless, hundreds of others would hurry to reserve hotel rooms in Reno and elsewhere beyond the TV blackout to watch the game.

DOWN TO THE WIRE 49ers 27, Packers 20

The 49ers entered week 12, knowing they were one of three teams (along with Baltimore and Detroit) with 7-4 records going into the final game of the season. Earlier in the day, the Rams eliminated the Colts, while the Lions beat the Bears. Now, only the Packers stood between the 49ers and a possible tie for the Western Division title.

With the Packers coming to town, two things were on the minds of the team and fans alike. First was the game itself. Second, Green Bay was hit by key injuries to its players who would not play in the final game.

It seemed the 49ers' major concern was not just the Packers but their injured quarterback, Y. A. Tittle. But the new legion of Brodie followers were positive he could direct the team to a win over the Packers.

His fans were rewarded and delighted when they found out he would be starting such a pivotal contest, as an overflow sellout crowd watched the 49ers jump out to a quick lead, 10-0, in the first quarter.

But it was short-lived. The Packers refused to quit, as quarterback Bart Starr directed the comeback, leading his team to a 20-10 halftime advantage.

Dreams of a 49er Western Division title seemed to be fading away. The team was in panic mode, but the spark that was needed for a victory was on the way.

A hobbling Tittle started the second half, and the fans went hysterical. Under his direction, the 49ers rallied for 20-20 tie as the third quarter ended. Then in the fourth quarter, Tittle's passing and Joe Perry's running produced a 69-yard drive for the winning touchdown. Detroit had downed the Bears 21-13 to gain a playoff with the 49ers.

Over the course of the 12 regular season games played in 1957, the 49ers would score 260 points—the fourth highest offensive output in the 12-team league.

Though on December 22, 1957, the dream ended. The 49ers, famous for fantastic comebacks, were the victim of a furious Detroit comeback.

Trailing 27-7 in the third quarter, and their starting quarterback, Bobby Layne, knocked out of the game, the courageous Lions, led by Tobin Rote, roared back to win 31-27, killing all hopes of a 49er championship.

The loss was devastating for everyone. Many fans call that day "a day that will live in infamy" for the 49ers' team and its fans. The 49ers lived by the sword during the 1957 season, and they died by it.

The following week, Detroit defeated Cleveland 59-14 in the NFL championship game. That game left many 49ers' fans asking that infamous question, "What if?"

49ers fans were demoralized after the loss. Judging by the articles in the newspapers the day after the game, the loss was the sports story of the "roller coaster" 49ers' season. The writers' antidote to our feelings of helplessness and malaise, instead, was to praise the 49ers' 1957 team.

"We lived in legendary days of Y. A. Tittle, Hugh McElhenny, Joe Perry, Bob St. Clair, Leo Nomellini," said Brachman of the San Francisco Examiner.

The only thing I can tell you is that while witnessing these games, I spent most of them on my feet, with my mouth agape, not because we kept scoring, but because it was so darn exciting. Indeed, it was a "wild ride to the finish," as once again the 49ers' fans began to chant "Wait 'til next year!" I knew what that meant.

34

Retribution

The nightmare second half of the 1957 divisional playoff game, when the Detroit Lions roared back for a 31-27 victory, was still vivid in the memories of all who witnessed the carnage. That day in December, the Lions came in like lambs, and they left like Lions. Our defense collapsed in the second half, and we played conservatively. We could not stop the five-foot-nine Tom "The Bomb" Tracy, the Lion's little-used halfback, nor their backup quarterback, Tobin Rote.

To this day, that loss brings up bitter memories. I can only remember how happy everyone was at halftime when we were ahead 24-7.

Jubilant 49ers' fans were celebrating, getting drunk, and talking about buying tickets to the expected NFL title game at Kezar against the mighty Jim Brown and the Cleveland Browns, who had won the Eastern Division title.

While most of the gloom was attributed to the final score, more than 50 spectators were overcome by food poisoning. Then to add insult to injury, Joe Perry broke his jaw in the third quarter of the game. The only thing left for the 49ers' faithful to look forward to was a rematch with the Lions in 1958, with the hope for a better ending.

That rematch came on November 2, 1958, as the Lions and the 49ers would once again square off in an important Western Conference game.

The 49ers had significant revenge on their minds, and this time the 49ers intended to be not disgraced by defeat but victorious.

The Lions were coming off a spectacular walloping of the Rams, 41-24, in Los Angeles, as Rote threw for three touchdowns. Surprisingly, the 49ers were installed as three-point favorites, mostly on the revenge factor.

Detroit was coming in with basically the same culprits who decimated the 49ers in the 1957 playoffs. Led by All-Pro linebackers Joe Schmidt and Alex Karras and tackles Lou Creekmor and Gil Mains, they had held the explosive Jon Arnett and the Rams' offense to only 45 yards rushing a week earlier. This was not favorable news for the 49ers' offense.

A crowd of 59,213 boisterous fans showed up for the game, and with Joe Perry pumped up full of 100-plus octane, the 49ers rallied to defeat the Lions 24-21. That day, Perry broke the 49ers' team single-game rushing record with 174 yards (currently the ninth most in team history).

The "Jet" blasted his way through the Lions' defense for long gains of 73- and 61-yard runs, as Hugh McElhenny's catch of a Y. A. Tittle screen-pass turned into a 32-yard broken-field run in the fourth quarter for a touchdown, which secured the win for the 49ers. The 1950s' most feared "threesome"—Tittle, Perry and McElhenny—were all at their explosive best. Anything less would have not have been suitable against the World Champion Lions.

Before halftime, a unique 49ers' play excited the hometown crowd, as placekicker Gordy Soltau attempted a free kick with 15 seconds remaining in the half. The field goal attempt was set up when

McElhenny had made a fair catch of Yale Lary's punt on the 49ers' 39-yard line. By NFL rules, a kick was permissible from any place on the field after a fair catch. Soltau's kick went off to the right side. The 49ers led 17-7 at the break and would continue their dominance in the second half.

It was also an afternoon of firsts. Much-heralded rookie halfback, Jim Pace, finally got to start a game and contributed in a big way. His 34-yard run was a dazzler and a touchdown builder.

Pace, a rookie out of Michigan, ended his most productive day as a 49er, with 58 yards rushing on 15 carries. The defense did its parts as well, playing in one of its best games of the season, as Matt Hazeltine made two outstanding defensive plays; without such, the 49ers would not have survived. Standing out were players on both sides of the ball, something that went beyond what the capacity crowd witnessed during the season.

As always, the 49ers had to do it the hard way, dominating in total yards as well: 411 yards to 171. An ineffective John Brodie started the game and completed 12 of 22 attempts for a mere 102 yards and was picked off three times in just three quarters-plus of action. Coach Albert made a tough decision to bench Brodie in favor of Tittle.

Suddenly, there was a stir in the tightly packed stands at Kezar, even with just the mere sight of the "Colonel" warming up on the sidelines.

The 49ers trailed 21-17 with just 11 minutes left in the game; a comeback would be tough, especially with turnovers aiding in Detroits' comeback. The hometown faithful were hoping that this game would not be a repeat of last year's playoff travesty.

With his arm loosened and ready for action, Tittle trotted off the bench to a tremendous cheer from the 49er faithful. This was his first action since suffering a groin injury in Chicago a month before.

Back at the controls, his mere presence gave the team and fans a big lift. He was, of course, "The Colonel," coming to lead the 49ers out of the wilderness of another defeat. And the feeling among the players on the field, as they expressed themselves pointedly, was that Tittle would get them out of trouble.

The 49ers had confidence in the young Brodie, but Tittle was the one who had experience with his knowledge of the game and right arm, and he was ready to not disappoint the fans. Just two plays after Tittle came in, the 49ers faced an annoyingly chronic situation: third down and seven.

(Author's note: Back in 1955, the 49ers had almost an exact situation against the Lions, when Tittle had suckered Jim David of the Lions' secondary on a hook-and-go pass; it had worked for a touchdown.)

The combination of Tittle to McElhenny came through again, as defensive back Jim David was faked out on the play. The play went for 33 yards, placing the ball on the 49er 32-yard line. It was déjà vu all over again.

Two plays later, Tittle pitched a screen pass to McElhenny, and he made a cut towards the center of the field. Aided by key blocks by Carl Rubke and John Gonzaga, he swerved directly away from two defenders but head-on towards two others; seven would-be Lions' tacklers would attempt to stop McElhenny, but he side-stepped away with his change-of-pace running, eventually scoring the go-ahead touchdown.

On the drive, Tittle had taken the 49ers 71 yards in six plays that was capped off by McElhenny's score. The Lions had fought right back to score an apparent go-ahead touchdown, sending the 49ers to certain defeat, but an offside penalty was called on Creekmur, the oldest tackle in the NFL at the time, and the play was nullified.

With just under two minutes left in the game, the Lions tried a 46-yard field goal, which was wide to the left, as it would have tied the score.

With the ball now in the 49ers' possession, and aided by a 19-yard run by Perry, the 49ers managed to run out the clock and preserve the victory. On this day, the 49ers needed a 60-minute team effort from its starters on offense and defense to win this one.

A jubilant McElhenny downplayed his contribution after the game saying, "It was a total team effort. Y. A. is a natural leader, but the "Jet" was the man today!" So excited, in fact, was Tittle, he gave sole credit for preserving the game, rightfully so, to Perry after the game. "Justifiably so!" said Albert. "Y. A., Perry and Mac gave us the offense we needed today, and the defense was outstanding. It was a great win for the team!"

35

Pearl Harbor Day

It was 17 years ago to the day on December 7, 1941, that the Japanese Imperial Navy surprised and attacked our U.S. Pacific Fleet at Pearl Harbor, Hawaii. This unprovoked attack was recalled by our country's Franklin D. Roosevelt, as his chilling words have been echoed down through the years: "A day which will live in infamy."

That action was one that would ultimately draw the United States into World War II.

Then, exactly 17 years to the day in 1958, the 49ers attacked the Green Bay Packers, as 50,792 jubilant hometown fans watched their heroes bomb the "enemy" (48-21) in a rout.

The 49ers launched a 27-point first-quarter scoring spree and never looked back. The first quarter mark and final tally equaled the 49ers all-time highs that were established in a 1952 game against the Texans.

The 49ers' fifth win of the season amounted to little more than a good calisthenic warm-up for the following Sunday's season finale against the Champion Baltimore Colts. The scoring spree against the Packers was one for the books for both teams.

First, Green Bay coming in to the game had its worst record in 40 years at 3-8. And for the exultant 49ers, the highlights would come from basically two players: Y. A. Tittle and halfback J. D. Smith.

Tittle would toss three touchdown passes—all in less than a quarter of action, while Smith's 80-yard scamper would place his mark alongside of Hugh McElhenny. Smith's run would be the fourth highest in the annals of 49ers' accomplishments, behind three of "The King's" runs of 89, 86 and 82 yards.

Turnovers by the Packers would play a large part of the onslaught: five interceptions and a fumble recovery. The five picks were a record by the 49ers' team at the time. All of this would aid in the Packers' ninth loss of the season, as all of this would take place even before the teams changed ends of the field for the second quarter.

It was a huge day for Billy Wilson, Perry, McElhenny, Tittle, and some of the other old guards, who called it a day after the fourth touchdown and sat down to watch their understudies finish off the job.

John Brodie, in relief of Tittle, wasn't having one of his better days, although he performed admirably, completing 16 of 23 passes for 162 yards. One pass to receiver Bill Jessup covered 26 yards and netted a touchdown.

But it was Tittle who started the game and immediately zeroed in on the Packer secondary, connecting on five of his first seven passes for 104 yards and three touchdowns. Part of the 49ers' scoring record was preserved by alert circus catches of Gordy Soltau, rookie Fred Dugan and Jessup.

It had been years since Soltau, the aging veteran, enjoyed himself as he did that day. He latched on to five receptions to head the list of nine different receivers who contributed in the game.

Looking back at all the fireworks in the game, perhaps the play of the day was the last one, in which rookie defensive back Abe

Woodson—a sprinter from Illinois—ran past would-be tacklers, following a kickoff return of 44 yards. The way the Packers were throwing the football, I had begun to wonder if they were mistaking the scarlet jerseys of the 49ers for the white ones of their own.

In the first quarter with Bart Starr on the firing line, defensive back Jim Ridlon intervened on the game's opening play with an interception at the Packer 48-yard line. Just two plays later, Tittle gave it a double windup, suckered Packer defender Billy Kinard out of position, and dropped a perfect pass in Wilson's arms at the Packer nine-yard line, good for a 44-yard gain.

Highlighting the 49ers' first-quarter action were five more running plays, including McElhenny's 21-yard dash and Perry's two-yard plunge into the end zone, putting the 49ers up 14-0.

Another Starr under-thrown pass was thrown directly at Bob Toneff, who rumbled back five yards to the Green Bay 10-yard line. Tittle lost no time in throwing a diagonal pass to Conner for a three-yard touchdown.

But the 49ers hadn't run out of the Christmas spirit quite yet, as Leo Nomellini broke through the line and disrupted the Packers' backup quarterback, Babe Parelli. He went flying in one direction, the ball in the other, as Nomellini's ferocious hit caused a fumble, and defensive end Ed Henke pounced on the ball at the Packer 47.

From there, in a matter of just five plays, the 49ers marched in for another score. Perry ran for 18 yards, then caught a Tittle pass for 17 yards. R. C. Owens caught one for 12 yards before Wilson faked out a Packer defensive back into easy submission and accepted a Tittle 22-yard pass for the final touchdown of the first quarter to up the score to 27-0.

The 49ers finished off their scoring in the third quarter after an impressive 40-yard punt return by Woodson. The 49ers used 10 plays, culminated by Jimmy Pace's five-yard scoring run.

The two NFL rivals would combine for over 800 yards of total offense, as San Francisco tallied 468 yards and the Packers, 335. Smith led all 49er rushers with 113 yards on 7 carries; Pace had 40 yards on 11 carries; McElhenny 25 yards on four carries; and Perry 28 yards on three carries. Soltau was the day's leader in receptions with five, followed by Dugan and Jessup with four catches each.

Head coach Frankie Albert was impressed with his defense in this game, especially with rookie defensive back Jerry Mertens. He had proven to be one of the finest defensive backs to come along for the 49ers in a long time. He had his hands full in defending Billy Howton, the best Packer receiver. And though Howton had out-maneuvered Mertens a couple of times, the rookie would not let it bother him.

The coaches of both the 49ers and Packers were unanimous on one thing following the game: the Packers were hopelessly out of the game within the first six minutes, but they continually battled the 49ers up to the final gun.

I'm still pondering the fact: If the 49ers had played all season long with the same fire as they did that day, where would the 49ers have ended up? Give me a couple of Tittles, a couple of McElhennys, St. Clairs, Toneffs, and a few Perrys and Wilsons or Soltaus to make up a team, full of men with desire and determination—we'd had a championship team.

36

A Fitting Farewell

Frankie Albert resigned as head coach of the 49ers on December 11, 1958, and I was not too surprised, but I had a generous measure of regret, as I thought he might quit.

Win, lose or tie, Albert would coach his last 49er game at Kezar against the 9-1 Colts. After the game, he would not remain with the club in any other official capacity. His decision to quit was as irrevocable as the day his decision was made.

Albert was under immense strain during the 1958 season, and his players knew it. But he never did show his feelings much, considering the circumstances under which he was working. It had been a disappointing season for everyone, and Albert did the best job he knew how to do.

And if the 49ers could pull off the upset in this game, they would have finished at 6-6, only two games off the previous season's playoff team. Incentives were numerous for both teams, which had a strange pregame pattern of favoritism.

The Colts were the most powerful offensive machine with 369 points, as contrasted with the 49ers' 236. Baltimore started out the week as 14-point favorites but entered the game even money, as far as the bookies were concerned. Two weeks prior to this game in Baltimore, the Colts had wiped out a 49er 27-7 lead, rallying to win 35-27.

Presumably, the odds makers were putting stock by the oldest existing hex in pro ball, the fact that no Colt team had ever beaten the 49ers at Kezar. That extended back to 1946, a span of 10 games.

Colts' head coach, Web Ewbank, said the Colts would "play hard," in deference to an expected sellout crowd in excess of 59,000 fans.

While Ewbank had refused to pay any heed to the Kezar jinx, his players were anxious to put an end to it. The Colts' Marchetti wanted nothing more than to break that streak.

"I'm not going to stand up and let the 49ers make me look bad. It's a matter of pride for me that my team winds up the regular season on a winning note before going into the playoffs," said Marchetti.

Entering the contest, Johnny Unitas had thrown for a league record of a touchdown in 24 straight games. He had a supporting cast that led the team's comeback against 49ers in Baltimore. Alan Ameche, the NFL's second-leading ground gainer, and the spectacular Lenny Moore, with a 73-yard sprint, each played a vital part in the Colts' comeback triumph over the 49ers in Baltimore. Plus, the Colts had lost only once during the season by three points, 24-21, to the Giants.

Witnessing the game, I would have thought the 49ers were playing for a world championship instead of just attempting to make their record come out a respectable 6-6 for the season against, admittedly, superior forces.

The manner in which this game would be played was inconceivable. They played the Colts as if they were possessed, as well as a team that had seemingly had its morale crushed after their head coach informed the team that he was quitting prior to the finale.

I would have thought the 49ers could have easily thrown in the towel and put off all winning endeavors until next season, but they did not.

The 49ers used all this negativity as an emotional spur. The old pros on the team—Tittle, McElhenny, Perry, St. Clair, Soltau, Wilson and Nomellini—rose up to the challenge. I believe it was really the factor that made the difference that game. Brilliant passing by Y. A. Tittle, stellar receiving by Clyde Conner, Billy Wilson, and R. C. Owens, and stunning power running by the seldom-used J. D. Smith all shared honors.

It turned out to be a valiant team effort by the 49ers. Tittle, despite a Colts' pass rush, which on numerous occasions threatened to bury him six feet under, finished off his season's work by completing 24 of 36 passes for 241 yards.

His ninth touchdown pass of the season was an eight-yarder to Conner in the second quarter to put the 49ers ahead to stay at 7-3. That was one of eight receptions by Conner, who in his third season as a 49er would latch on to a team-high of 49 catches. The 49ers' defense was astounding also—holding the No. 1 offensive team to only 12 first downs, two by rushing. San Francisco outgained the Colts, 368 to 289.

The defense held Baltimore's star backfield to season lows as well. Unitas was held to only 14 completions, while fullback Ameche, who was selected instead of Perry to represent the West in the Pro Bowl, was limited to just 14 total net rushing yards. Perry led all 49ers' rushers with 50 yards on seven attempts.

The turning point in the game came in the third quarter. With the 49ers leading by a slim 7-6 score, it was the capacity crowd that seemed to call the play, which brought about the 49ers' second touchdown and enabled Albert to close out the books with a victory.

However, were it not for the 49ers' faithful fans' input, the 49ers might not have made it. Certainly, Albert was going to try something else. Then the crowd took over and forced Albert to change his mind.

All of this transpired in the third quarter with the 49ers coming up to a fourth down and three-to-go situation on the Colts 21-yard line. In Albert's judgment, the circumstances called for a field goal. Looking toward the west end of the bench, he motioned to Gordy Soltau into the game. He had already missed a 30-yard field goal from the 30, had another blocked from the 49, and was wide on a hurried 50-yard attempt just before the half ended.

Soltau didn't get very far. He had taken only four or five strides toward the 49er huddle, when a protesting roar from the crowd all but rocked Albert off his feet. The 49ers didn't go for the field goal. Albert motioned for Soltau back to the bench, as the grandstand fans got their way.

McElhenny then took a pitch out and made an 11-yard run against the NFL's best defensive line, picking up a much-needed first down at the Colts' 10-yard line. Four plays later, halfback Smith crashed over the goal line for the touchdown. That huge touchdown pretty well determined the outcome of the game. With it, the 49ers went ahead with a 14-6 lead, giving the team the advantage where another touchdown or a pair of field goals wouldn't be enough for the Colts to battle back.

The last 49ers' score was a thing of beauty. In the fourth quarter, Tittle had completed two straight passes to Wilson for 13 and 7 yards and then faked the shoes off the Colts to maneuver the payoff.

Tittle, faking a handoff, which had everybody in the place thinking Perry had the ball, whirled out of the pocket and to his left. It was soft pickings as Tittle dropped a pass into the arms of Conner. He did an artistic job maneuvering free, leaving the closest Colt 10 yards behind for the 22-yard score.

The Colts added two insignificant fourth quarter Steve Myra field goals to close out the scoring, as the 49ers upset Baltimore, 21-12.

When the final gun sounded, Kezar came unglued. The faithful threw paper. They waved their arms. They spilled beer on each other. They chanted, "WE'RE NUMBER ONE! WE'RE NUMBER ONE!" The enthusiasm of several thousand spectators overflowed onto the playing field and soon got out of hand, and they brought down the goal posts.

A near riot broke out, and it took a battalion of police rushing to the stadium for an hour to restore order. In the midst of it all, Bob St. Clair braved life and limb, as he dove into the middle of the milling crowd to rescue the game ball. He later turned it over to Albert in the dressing room. It was the end of a long season and a fitting farewell to Albert—carpe diem.

In retrospect, there was some evidence that Albert was running the West Coast-style offense during the1958 season. The 49ers finished first in completion percentage and in the middle of the pack in yards per completions. That season, Tittle completed 57.7 percent of his passes and 7.1 yards per toss (ninth in the league), while Brodie completed 59.9 percent. Together, they had 118 completions to their backs and flanker and 141 to their ends.

37

Hula Bowl Showcased 49ers

The Hula Bowl is a story of two energetic young men, Mackay Yanagisawa, a Honolulu businessman, and Paul Stupin of Los Angeles, who set out on a goal to bring the very best players available from the mainland to the Hawaiian Islands. The first competing teams were the Hawaiian All-Stars made up of graduates of Leiehua High School in Wahiawa against a squad of college All-Stars from the mainland.

A notable college All-Star and Hawaiian native was Herman Wedemeyer, nicknamed "Squirmin' Herman," who went to St. Mary's college in California, earning All-American honors and a stint with the 49ers.

Many players whose schools did not make the New Year's Day bowl games hoped for invitations to the North-South, Senior Bowl, Shriner's East-West, or the Blue-Gray game. But a majority of the players chose an invitation to Hawaii to play in the Hula Bowl, as was their ultimate choice.

And the big names started coming with a lineup of football greats unmatched anywhere. Sponsors of the Hula Bowl scheduled the games on a date after all the other bowl games had been played, thereby making it possible for participating players in these games to make the trip to Hawaii.

During the Golden Age era, the Hula Bowl Committee scheduled two games between the Hawaiians and the College All-Stars each January, to be played at the Honolulu Stadium at King Street and Isenberg Street. The 26,000-seat stadium was Honolulu's premier gathering place. It was nostalgic. It had the classic ballpark aroma, with added Hawaiian delicacies too, like pipikaula and manapua served at the games.

In 1951, the format changed to allow NFL players to join the Hawaiian All-Stars, in an effort to create a more competitive environment.

Almost instantly, with the addition of big name pro stars, the game received national attention. Before long, the game represented more than a half dozen consensus All-American players and future 49ers participants: Wedemeyer (St. Mary's), Gordy Soltau (Minnesota), Hugh McElhenny (Washington), Leo Nomellini (Minnesota), Matt Hazeltine (California), Dickey Moegle (Rice), Harry Babcock (Georgia), St. Clair (Tulsa-49ers), Billy Wilson (San Jose State), Jerry Tubbs (Oklahoma), and Charlie Krueger (Texas A & M) all played for the College All-Stars.

And players from the 49ers' pro ranks came: Joe Perry, Y. A. Tittle, R. C. Owens, Frankie Albert, Bob Toneff, Clyde Conner, Carroll Hardy, and Joe Arenas joined forces with the Hawaiian All-Stars. These and many others 49ers played in the Hula Bowl during, or just before, their glory years in the NFL.

With a cornucopia of talent, the 1951 Hula Bowl became the scene of many dramatic moments. Hugh McElhenny, a rookie out of Washington (and the 49ers' No. 1 draft pick in 1952), had dazzled the crowd in the game, with a 53-yard touchdown run, averaging

20 yards per carry and leading the College All-Stars to a 41-40 cliff-hanger victory.

Quarterback Frankie Albert, playing with the Hawaiians, was so impressed with McElhenny that he called 49ers' coach, Buck Shaw, after the game. He told Shaw to draft that kid because McElhenny was the most talented halfback he'd ever seen.

By 1956, the Hula Bowl All-Star Football Classic had proven to be one of the most exciting of all the postseason All-Star games. College stars from 13 different universities across the nation, including 10 team captains from eight major conferences and five bowl games, plus selected NFL stars, made the game the biggest attraction in Hawaii's long and colorful grid history.

At the end of the decade, the Hula Bowl had invited over 450 players from 71 different colleges and universities from coast to coast, representing every major conference and bowl game, and 110 players from 12 NFL teams.

Historically over the nine-year period (1951-1959), the Hula Bowl became one of the nation's biggest attractions among the nation's top postseason games, including the Pro Bowl and the Pro Champions vs. College All-Stars.

"Fun" seemed to be the key word from the 49ers' past performers recollections:

"Playing in Hawaii was simply fun," said Hugh McElhenny. "Besides the game, I enjoyed the beautiful weather, the beaches and playing a round of golf in Honolulu."

"You can make money, but you can't manufacture the memories playing at the Hula Bowl," said Matt Hazeltine, who played center for the College All-Stars. "The games were colorful. Everybody had fun over there. I got in my share of sightseeing in, and overall, I had an excellent time."

"Playing there was a real treat. The first time I saw the stadium, I was in awe. The place was jammed with marching bands, balloons were blowing in the trade winds, and the big 'volcano' float during halftime was spectacular," said an ecstatic Y. A. Tittle.

Clyde Conner said of his first trip to Hawaii: "The trip for my family and I to the Islands, and their warm hospitality, was the best. I won't forget those hula girls, who gave us leis around our necks."

Dickey Moegle recalled, "I was only 19 years old, and I shut down the Rams' end, 'Crazy Legs' Hirsch playing with the Hawaiians. He didn't catch a pass on me. They put that out on the AP (Associated Press) wire, and I remember people saying, 'Who is that guy?'"

"Everyone had fun over there," stated R. C. Owens, who played with the Hawaiians. "It's nice to play together with other players with different cultures. It's an experience I'll never forget."

"I broke my shoulder at the beginning of the 1957 season, and I wasn't expected to play in the Hula Bowl, but I did," said Bob St. Clair.

"Playing with those servicemen from Pearl Harbor and Hickam Field was a real honor. Every time we got the ball, we scored; it was 35-0 in the first quarter! After the game, we ran across the field to the liquor store and bought a bunch of beer. The next day, teammate Frank Gifford tried teaching me how to water ski at Waikiki. It wasn't my kind of sport."

49ers 1950s Hula Bowl Squad Members

First team College All-Stars:
1951: Hugh McElhenny, HB (Washington)

1957: Jerry Tubbs, C (Oklahoma)

Second team College All-Stars:
1955: Carroll Hardy, HB (Colorado)

First team pros:

    1952: Y. A. Tittle, QB

    1955: Hugh McElhenny, HB

    1956: Leo Nomellini, DT

Second team pros:

    1954: Joe Arenas, HB

    1956: Matt Hazeltine, C

38

Pro Bowlers

The 49ers had quite the history in the NFL's postseason Pro Bowl game during the Golden Age of Pro football, with some of the franchise's most notable players making an impact in the annual contest.

After the 1950 NFL season, the All-Star game, dubbed the Pro Bowl, was composed of players from the American Conference, which represented the East, and the National Conference, which represented the West. This format only lasted only a few years until 1954, when the Pro Bowl committee changed its format to the Eastern Conference vs. Western Conference for the remainder of the decade.

The games were played in sunny Southern California at the Los Angeles Memorial Coliseum. The personnel of the All-Pro teams, some 60 players in all, were named by the coaches and writers, and each had used extreme knowledge in their selections. Once selected, the All-Star players were labeled the "blue-ribbon" athletes of the NFL.

In those days the annual Pro Bowl was not considered an exhibition game, as players in each conference had little use for each other, and vice versa. It was an honor for a player to be chosen to represent his conference. The Pro Bowl was the equivalent to a major-league baseball All-Star game and as popular as the Shriners East-West College All-Star game, according to national TV ratings.

The American Conference won the first-ever Helms Athletic Pro Bowl Trophy with a 28-27 win over the National Conference on January 14, 1951. With 53,676 in attendance, Browns' quarterback, Otto Graham, threw for three scores and won the first George Halas Trophy for the game's outstanding player.

In 1953, the 49ers sent a total of seven players to the Pro Bowl. The initial score of the game came when tackle Leo Nomellini sacked Graham and recovered his fumble in the first quarter. This set up the first of McElhenny's two touchdowns to lead the National Conference to a 27-7 victory.

The 1955 Pro Bowl could have easily been called the 49ers Pro Bowl. 49ers head coach Buck Shaw coached the Western Conference squad.

Before 42,972 cheering fans, Y. A. Tittle completed 16 of 26 passes and threw two touchdowns, most of them to teammate end, Billy Wilson, who had a record 11 receptions for 157 yards and one touchdown. Perry finished the scoring with a three-yard touchdown run for the West in a 26-19 win. Wilson won the George Halas MVP Trophy.

An elated Shaw commented after the big win, "Being together with all these great players for a week was a new experience. Well, what else does one do in Los Angeles, for if not to have fun and play football!"

Led by Y. A. Tittle and Hugh McElhenny, the 49ers again made a huge impact in the 1958 Pro Bowl. The West team dominated this game with 66,634 fans showing up to set a new Pro Bowl attendance record, as the West defense held the East to a mere 149 total yards, also a record. The West won the game 26-7, and McElhenny took home the George Halas Trophy, being selected MVP.

By the end of the decade, the Pro Bowl game had become an important fixture each year on the winter sports schedule in Southern California, as much as the Rose Bowl and the Los Angeles Open Golf Tournament.

49ers Pro Bowlers in the decade:

1950:
Frankie Albert, QB
Visco Grgich, LB
Leo Nomellini, DT
Norm Standlee, FB
John Stzykalski, HB

1951:
Jimmy Cason, DB
Ray Collins, OT
Leo Nomellini, DT
Gordy Soltau, E

1952:
Hardy Brown, LB
Ed Henke, DE
Bill Johnson, C
Hugh McElhenny, HB
Leo Nomellini, DT
Joe Perry, FB
Gordy Soltau, E

1953:
Bill Johnson, C
Hugh McElhenny, HB
Art Michalik, G
Leo Nomellini; DT
Joe Perry, FB
Gordy Soltau, E
Y. A. Tittle, QB

1954:
Bruno Banducci, G
Al Carapella, DT
Jimmy Cason, DB
John Henry Johnson, HB
Joe Perry, FB
Y. A. Tittle, QB
Billy Wilson, E

1955:
Dickey Moegle, DB
Bob Toneff, T
Billy Wilson, E

1956:

Hugh McElhenny, HB
Leo Nomellini, DT
Bob St. Clair, T
Billy Wilson, E

1957:

Marv Matuszak, LB
Hugh McElhenny, HB+
Leo Nomellini, DT
Y. A. Tittle, QB
Billy Wilson, E

1958:

Hugh McElhenny, HB
Jerry Mertens, DB
Leo Nomellini, DT
Bob Clair, T
Billy Wilson, E

1959:

Dave Baker, DB
Leo Nomellini, DT
Bob St. Clair, T
J. D. Smith, FB
Billy Wilson, E
Abe Woodson, DB
+MVP

49ers Pro Bowl Records:

Passing:

Completions career: 40, Y. A. Tittle (1954, 1955, 1958)
Completions game: 16, Y. A. Tittle (1955)
Touchdown passes career: 2, Y. A. Tittle (1955)

Receptions:

Billy Wilson: 11 (1955)

Scoring:

Points career: 18, Hugh McElhenny (1953, 1959)
Points game: 12, Hugh McElhenny (1953)
Touchdowns career: 3, Hugh McElhenny (1953, 1959)

39

Ballers of the Hardwood

The 1957 49ers will always be remembered for their thrilling "cliff-hangers" and fabulous comebacks and a tie for first place with Detroit, as each team finished the Western Conference with an identical 8-4 record.

It was after a disappointing playoff loss to the Lions that a group of 49er players decided to trade in their football gear for basketball togs and shoes in the off-season. Beginning in January of 1958, eight members of the team played 30 exhibition basketball games, barnstorming the West Coast and Canada.

Ten of those games were against the Harlem Globetrotters. The balance of games was played against the Rams' players and some college teams, featuring coaches and alumni. Games were played mostly in the Bay Area, in San Francisco, Oakland, San Jose, Santa Rosa, Gillroy, Stockton, El Cerrito, Milpitas, Alamo, and far away as Vancouver, Canada.

"Still, we had to make due," Gordy Soltau said. "We usually had to cover our own traveling expenses. While another teammate, Billy Wilson, supplied us the uniforms from his sporting goods store.

"The team was a very competitive team and took their games seriously. We had a lot of guys with great coordination and skillful ball handling," said the six foot three R. C. "Alley-Oop" Owens, who played forward and toured Europe in the spring with the Seattle Buckann Bakers.

"Our team had balance. Owens could outjump almost anybody," said five foot nine Joe Arenas, who played guard and was the team's playmaker. Arenas had enrolled at Nebraska on a basketball scholarship, so he knew the game very well.

Clyde Conner, at six foot two, played guard and was an outstanding basketball player at the College of Pacific, while six foot nine Bob St. Clair was the tallest player of the group and played center. He brought his Poly High School basketball toughness to the team.

Wilson was a six foot four multi-talented athlete, who played forward at San Jose State and was one of the team's top scorers, while Soltau, six foot two, could shoot and rebound well and handled the finances of the team.

Hugh McElhenny at six foot one was a pretty good ball handler too. Ed Henke, six foot four, was called "Frank Buck," because he'd rather fish and hunt than play basketball, but they needed him to fill the roster. Y. A. Tittle at six foot, who fancied himself as a basketball player, was also on the team.

"We went undefeated in its first eight games, until we lost a close game, 56-48, to the Globetrotters at the Cow Palace, in front of a sold-out crowd of 15,000," Owens added. "In addition, we played them in San Jose, Sacramento, Fresno, Santa Barbara, Portland, Yakima, Seattle, Spokane and Vancouver."

"The Harlemites (Globetrotters) claimed all its exhibitions games against us were 'real competitive' contests," said St. Clair. "The pay was pretty good too, and we earned as much as $200 a game when we played them. Unfortunately, we never could beat them. We played 'em tough every game."

St. Clair even had a moment with a future NBA Hall of Famer on the hardwood. "Owner Abe Saperstein told me not to rough up their star player: seven foot center Wilt Chamberlin, because Wilt was their big draw," St. Clair said. "Well, after taking a few of his elbows from his driving layups in the game, I gave him a warning to cool it with the elbows. Unfortunately for Wilt, he did it again, and I gave him a ferocious block that leveled him. He hit the hardwood flat on his back. He never elbowed me again.

"The following year, we toured Canada and played four games against the Globetrotters. I made some real good money then—$700 a game—far more than I ever did playing football that year."

Tittle, a basketball aficionado, called Soltau one day and said, "A team called the 'Hawks' wants to play us in Reno, Nevada. They would guarantee us $200 each and cover expenses."

Unfortunately, their trip didn't go as expected. Upon arrival at the Mapes Hotel and to the 49ers' players dismay, they noticed quite a few tall guys in the lobby. Then they were told these guys were members of the NBA Champion St. Louis Hawks. To make a long story short, the 49ers hoopsters were no match for them, as the Hawks ran away with the game.

"At halftime, their head coach, Alex Hannam, showed some compassion for us and offered us a compromise," Soltau said. "He would let us add some of his star players to our roster for the rest of the game. Ultimately, we avoided further embarrassment and played the second half even."

40

Other 49ers' Vets

When Tony Morabito selected Lawrence "Buck" Shaw as his head coach to lead San Francisco's first football franchise in1946, he delivered on his promise to bring the best coach on board.

Shaw had an extremely impressive résumé. He had an outstanding career as a tackle and placekicker at Notre Dame under Knute Rockne. At Santa Clara University, he coached a group of Broncos to back-to-back Sugar Bowl wins: a 21-14 win over the LSU Tigers in 1937, and he guided his undefeated Broncos (9-0) once again to a 6-0 victory over LSU in 1938. In addition, Shaw coached one season at California in1945 before leaving for San Francisco.

As coach of the 49ers, Shaw had only one losing season, in 1950, when he made the jump from the AAFC to the NFL. He was an offensive-minded coach and unfortunately never cared much about defense. Shaw had an overall winning record of 33 wins and 24 losses from 1950-54, but no championships. He did succeed in winning an NFL Championship in 1960 as coach of the Philadelphia Eagles.

John Riley Brodie was third in the line of the teams' great signal callers after Frankie Albert and Y. A. Tittle. At Stanford University, he led the entire nation in total offense and passing during his final season, and he was selected All-American in 1956. He was named the MVP of the 1957 East-West Game and the College All-Star Game.

Brodie was the team's first-round No. 1 selection in the 1957 NFL draft, following the selection of Notre Dame's Paul Hornung, (Packers) and USC's Jon Arnett (Rams).

A highlight of his debut season in the NFL came against the Colts at Kezar, as he hurled the game-winning touchdown pass to Hugh McElhenny with 40 seconds left in the game. Prior to the heroic toss, the 49ers' rookie had attempted only eight passes, connecting six times.

In his second season in the NFL, Brodie showed signs that he would be capable of leading the team over the next few years. He led the league in 1958 in completion percentage (59.9), hitting on 103 of 172 attempts.

From 1957-59, he competed with Tittle for playing time, until his youthful arm and his mobility trumped Tittle's age, his arm and lack of mobility.

During Brodie's 16-year career (1957-73), he led the league in passing yardage, passing touchdowns, least sacks, and lowest percentage of passes intercepted. He retired as the third most prolific career passer in NFL history, having been named the 1970 League MVP, as well as a two-time Pro Bowler. In the off-seasons, Brodie was a professional golfer from January to July, playing in several tournaments on the PGA circuit.

★ ★ ★ ★ ★ ★

The level of skill demonstrated by Matt Hazeltine was instantly recognized from the very beginning of training camp in 1955. Almost immediately, he won the job as the 49ers' starting outside linebacker.

He was accorded by head coach Frankie Albert as one of the best linebackers ever to adorn a 49ers' uniform. He was six foot,197 pounds, when he reported to the 49ers, but he rose to 220 pounds and retained his weight for the next 14 seasons, earning him the nickname "Iron Man" for his dedication, durability and his inspirational courage and play.

He was an All-American center for Pappy Waldorf at California in 1954. He was a two-time Pro Bowler and an esteemed member of the College Football Hall of Fame. The Matt Hazeltine "Iron Man Award" was named after his 13-year career. The award is given annually to the most courageous and inspirational defensive 49er player.

J. D. Smith could do it all. Around the NFL, he was called the "Cinderella Man." He was drafted by the Bears in 1956 but was dropped after six games before San Francisco signed him, as the team was in desperate need of a defensive back.

Actually, Red Hickey, then an assistant coach, had an idea that Smith would be more effective on offense, with his 207-pound frame and 9.7 timing in the 100-yard dash. But the needs of the moment took precedence, and he played on defense during the 1957 season.

Smith had times of acute frustration and despair, especially in the closing games of 1957, when 49er fans' booed lustily every time his name was announced over the public address system. The mistakes of a defensive back, especially when he permitted a receiver to get behind him, were all too apparent to the people in the stands. Hickey told Smith, "Just go out there and do your best. These same people booing you now will be cheering for you next year."

In 1958, with Joe Perry and Hugh McElhenny having excellent seasons, Smith spent most of the time on the bench, but he got those cheers predicted by Hickey when he ran 80 yards for a touchdown against the Packers.

Destiny took over for Smith at the beginning of 1959. Perry was set at fullback, but McElhenny was moved to flanker, and Jim Pace, who was expected to be the other halfback, was injured.

From then on, Smith found security as a halfback, as he became one of the few players in NFL history to gain more than 1,000 yards in a single season (1,036 to be exact). He carried the ball 207 times, an all-time 49er record at the time, but still 83 less than the league leader, Jim Brown of Cleveland. Smith had a slightly higher rushing per carry than the legendary Brown: 5.0 to 4.6.

For the season, Smith scored 10 touchdowns in only 14 regular season games, a mark that remains tied with six other 49er players for the team's standard, including Perry for the most rushing touchdowns ever in single-season team history.

Abe Woodson was the 49ers' No. 2 draft pick in 1957. His moves were not just limited to the gridiron, as he had twice tied the world record with his blazing speed in the 50-meter hurdles. The former Illinois All-American played on both sides of the ball while in college prior to becoming a 49er, where he would play defensive back and return kickoffs—highlighted by his 105-yard run back against the Rams, which remains the longest in team history. He would miss the 1957 49ers' playoff game because of a hitch in the Army. Surprisingly, during his seven-year career with the 49ers, the team never won more than seven games with Woodson in the lineup.

★ ★ ★ ★ ★ ★

Bill Johnson, six foot three, 240 pounds, was a mainstay at the center position for the 49ers (1948-56). His skills marked him as a physical wonder, as well as a student of the game. Nicknamed "The Tiger" by his teammates, he played at a level of the best centers of the decade.

They also had another nickname for him, "Mr. Anonymous," for the way he selflessly anchored the offensive line that cleared the way for the 49ers' "Million Dollar Backfield" of Tittle, McElhenny, Perry and Johnson. A two-time Pro Bowler, Johnson served as a 49ers' assistant coach in his last two seasons with the club.

Defensive end Ed Henke was a player willing to "pay the price." I'll always remember him for his valiant effort against the Bears at Kezar in 1957. In that game, he gave every ounce of his energy with his ferocious hits on Bears' quarterback, Ed Brown. His replacement, Zeke Bratowski, received the same harassment from Henke. On the game's final play, Henke collapsed from sheer exhaustion, while preserving a hard fought 21-17 victory by the 49ers.

At first, Howard "Red" Hickey was hired as a 49ers' assistant coach under head coach Red Strader in 1955. But after the team struggled through a 4-8 season, Strader was replaced by assistant coach Frankie Albert. Hickey stayed on as an assistant during the three years, as Albert handled the head coaching duties for the team.

In 1957, Hickey helped quarterback Tittle and flanker Owens develop the "alley-oop" pass play. When Albert resigned following the1958 season, Hickey was promoted to head coach.

During his first season in 1959, the 49ers put up a stiff challenge to the defending champion Colts, managing a tie for the Western Conference lead with two games to play. However, the Colts broke the deadlock with a 34-14 victory over the 49ers and went on to capture another NFL title.

In 1960-61, Hickey made three members of the famed "Million Dollar Backfield" (Tittle, Perry and McElhenny) expendable in favor of a three-quarterback shuttle service he devised, called the "shotgun offense."

Tittle was dealt to the Giants for guard/linebacker Lou Cordileone; Perry went to the Colts for a "conditional" third-round pick (though, Perry led the Colts' team in rushing with 675 yards and three touchdowns), whereas the conditions of the trade were unmet, and Baltimore did not relinquish a draft choice; McElhenny was left unprotected in the expansion draft, as Minnesota signed him while they began stocking players for their first team in 1961.

The three former stars all found success with their new teams. Cordileone, however, would only play one season for the 49ers and was traded to the Rams for second-year defensive back Elbert Kimbrough.

The multi-talented halfback, Carroll Hardy, played just one season with the team in 1955, while giving up a promising career with the 49ers to pursue a major league baseball career as an outfielder. He played eight seasons in the majors with five different clubs. Hardy is most recognized as the only major league player to ever pinch hit for Ted Williams in a major league game.

★ ★ ★ ★ ★ ★

Guard Bruno Banducci, one of the original players from the 49ers' inaugural season in 1946, tried to beat Father Time at the age of 35 in 1956. Starting his 20th season of football—three years of high school, four years at Stanford, two years with the Eagles, nine years with the 49ers, and one season in the CFL—all came to an abrupt end during the 1955 training camp, as Banducci did not make the final cut and retired.

Johnny Thomas was a great basketball talent. He was drafted as an offensive end, a "red-shirt" pick in 1956 as he never played the position, while with the 49ers. Instead, he played tackle and guard on offense and linebacker on the opposite side of the ball. He also enjoyed basketball and received a tryout with the NBA's St. Louis Hawks. During the winter of 1958, he barnstormed with Al "Runt" Pullins' Fabulous Harlem Clowns, previously known as the Broadway Clowns.

The highly recruited All-American quarterback Earl Morrall was drafted in the first round in 1956 by the 49ers. He was supposed to be the heir apparent quarterback to Y. A. Tittle. Instead, Morrall lasted just one season with the 49ers, as he and guard Mike Sandusky were traded to the Steelers for two first-round draft picks in the 1957 draft.

Morrall lasted another 21 years in the NFL, playing for six different teams. He passed for 20,809 yards and 161 touchdowns, earning him the title of the NFL's "greatest backup quarterback" ever. He appeared in three Super Bowls and was a two-time All-Pro and two-time Pro Bowler.

The 49ers used their No. 1 NFL draft pick (11th overall) in 1954 on the highly touted quarterback, B. J. "Bernie" Faloney. They offered Faloney $9,000 to play defensive back and backup quarterback to Tittle. However, the Edmonton Eskimos of the Canadian Football League outbid the 49ers for his services. Faloney accepted $12,500, and he headed north. Faloney, a scrambling quarterback, helped the Edmonton Eskimos to the 1954 Grey Cup title.

Harry Babcock had bad luck. The six-foot-two, highly recruited end came to the 49ers as a No. 1 "bonus choice" draft pick in 1953. After being selected All-American at Georgia, he would be invited to participate—and would star—in the Shriners East-West Game and also the Hula Bowl. Unfortunately, he severely hurt his leg in the College All-Star Game in Chicago prior to reporting to the 49ers. He saw only limited action his first season. And in 1954, a shoulder dislocation and a knee injury occurred in a preseason game against the Cardinals. This was the crowning blow to his short career with the team that lasted just two seasons.

Just three seasons into his career with the 49ers (1959-61), Dave Baker, an All-Pro cornerback, left the team at the prime of his career. At the time, Baker was only the second player in NFL history to record four interceptions in a game (vs. the Rams) in 1959.

He received his Army orders during the spring of 1962, and would be lost to the team for at least one, possibly two seasons. After he received his honorable discharge from the U.S. Army as a second lieutenant, Baker spurned the 49ers and accepted the position of athletic director and head basketball coach at Bethany Nazarene College for the next 10 years.

★ ★ ★ ★ ★ ★

Wally Yonamine, who played running back for the 49ers, was the first NFL player of Asian ancestry to play professional baseball in Japan after World War II. He signed with the Yomiuri Giants in 1951 and was inducted into Japan's Baseball Hall of Fame in 1994. His lone season in the NFL was 1947.

★ ★ ★ ★ ★ ★

One and done. Marv Matuzak played one full season (12 games) at linebacker for the 49ers, earning him All-Pro recognition in 1957. Four games into the 1958 season, he was released and signed with the Green Bay Packers.

41

The Opponents

My affection for the 49ers of the Golden Age will last until forever, though, there were some very intriguing formidable 49ers' opponents that I followed. I wanted to acknowledge them in my book because of their popularity and for their courageous performances.

Johnny Unitas of the Colts was my favorite quarterback over the decade. His throwing motion was uncanny—so accurate. He was flamboyant and he had style. He would take a normal three-step drop, half-cock his arm, feint one way, then look the other way. Then POW!—fire a bullet pass right on target. It was like poetry in motion. He wasn't very mobile, but he stayed in the pocket until the last second.

On the other hand, I really feared the "Dutchman," Norm Van Brocklin, from the Rams. What a passer he was. Like Tittle, he could thread the needle. He was so terrific at throwing the bomb. I'd call them missiles.

He would just drop back and fire 50- to 60-yard strikes with such ease. (Of course, he had two Hall of Famers, Tommy Fears and Elroy Hirsch, and a speedster named Bob Boyd to throw to.)

One game in particular at Kezar in 1954, Nomellini nailed him with a big hit. Van Brocklin, who seldom could not resist baiting the 49ers into a brawl, jumped up, and took a swing at Nomellini. It was reported in the San Francisco Chronicle the next day that Van Brocklin had invited Nomellini to meet him outside after the game to settle the matter. Van Brocklin never showed up.

Otto Graham of the Browns was a different type of quarterback. Much like Tittle, he had great instincts and peripheral vision, and he always found his target. I remember in a preseason game at Kezar in 1956, with George Ratterman at quarterback for the Browns, that we dominated them. A few weeks later, the Browns and 49ers hooked up again in a regular season contest. Graham started the game and passed us silly in a 38-3 rout.

The most fun to watch was little Eddie LeBaron of the Redskins. He was supposed to be too short for the NFL, but at five foot seven, 160 pounds, little Eddie played like a "giant." I would compare him to Frankie Albert, who could befuddle anybody.

LeBaron was daring, clever, elusive, unpredictable and smart. Often, I'd have to wait for the play to unfold, before I could get a glimpse of his unnerving unorthodox style. I never knew if he was going to roll out and throw a jump pass or keep it on a bootleg around the end. He always put on a show.

Buddy Young of the Colts was my favorite opposing halfback. He was only five foot four, smallest in the NFL, and yet he was faster than Perry. Young was also versatile. He ran the ball, caught screen passes and returned punts. His size was not a disadvantage, and he always seemed to outsmart us and made us look foolish at times.

I always liked Ollie Matson, who was drafted ahead of McElhenny in 1952. Each time the Cardinals played to Kezar, Matson was bestowed with cheers from his local followers. And when he carried the ball, he was a constant threat to go all the way on sweeps. He used his Olympic sprinter speed to his advantage.

Watching Frank Gifford of the Giants was a bit like watching McElhenny in the open field. Not only was he a gifted runner, he caught passes and was a superb punt returner. Often, he would be called upon to throw the run-pass option, which always seemed to work against us. Without Gifford, I don't feel the Giants could have beaten us.

Jon Arnett, the swivel-hipped Ram, also reminded me of "The King," in the open field. He had a sixth sense. With a head fake and a change of direction, he was gone. He was quick to the hole like Perry. He was one of my favorite backs to watch.

Willie "The Wisp" Galimore of the Bears was like lightning in a bottle. He was so fast and elusive. To me, he was the first coming of

Gale Sayers. Unfortunately, his career was shortened due to an auto accident that claimed his life.

Harlon Hill of the Bears was a prime torturer of the 49ers. He was such a deep threat and always seemed to get open. A game I witnessed at Kezar in 1954 on Halloween turned out to be a nightmare for the 49ers. Hill terrified our defenders, catching four touchdown passes, the last one a 65-yard pass play in the final 0:25 seconds to beat us, 31-27.

Elroy "Crazy Legs" Hirsch of the Rams was like our Billy Wilson. He had good speed but not great speed. He had great hands like Wilson and ran his routes to perfection. When Hirsch was in the lineup, I knew we were in for a high-scoring game. People would ask me if I thought Hirsch's legs were really crazy. His legs were always gyrating in six different directions all at the same time.

The Colts' Raymond Berry was one of the greatest receivers I ever saw. He caught everything Unitas threw at him. He had great balance, and seldom did I see him drop a pass, while flanker Lenny Moore, also of the Colts, was a like a thoroughbred racehorse. He was swift, fast, and when Unitas let one fly deep, Moore was usually his intended target. He was called "Spats" because of the way he taped his high-top shoes.

Tom Fears of the Rams had the best moves. Considered a possession receiver without great speed, he was sure-handed and could separate from defenders on a dime. Time and time again, Van Brocklin and Fears hooked up for first downs on a regular basis. In my opinion, with Hirsch, Fears and Boyd in the lineup, the Rams possessed the best receiving corps of the decade.

And then there was Tommy McDonald of the Eagles. No single receiver had the enthusiasm that McDonald brought to the game. At five foot nine, 167 pounds, he would be considered tiny by today's standards, yet his athletic ability was undeniable. He made circus catches and seldom dropped a toss.

If any 49ers fan wanted to see a heavyweight brawl, they only had to watch the Colts' six foot four Gino Marchetti tangle with tackle Bob St. Clair. In a game played at Kezar in 1958, the soon-to-be-crowned World Champion Colts squared off with the 49ers, and St. Clair did not allow Marchetti one quarterback sack.

Another brawler was the Lions' Lou Creekmur, their six-foot-four, 250-pound offensive guard. According to Charley Powell, he was the toughest lineman he ever faced. When he battled Creekmur, it was a war. Before a game, Creekmur would wrap both hands fully in duct tape, as if he was getting ready for a prizefight. Powell himself was a professional boxing contender.

Another 49ers' nemesis was linebacker Sam Huff of the Giants. He was an outstanding linebacker. He was a bully, unrelenting, and he brought havoc to Tittle and Brodie and our backs. Perry once said Huff was like "poison" on giving a punch or taking a hit from him. He said he treated it as a mano a mano.

And lastly, Chicago Bears' head coach, George "Papa Bear" Halas. He had to be mentioned because of his entertaining antics on the field. No one coach displayed more animation than Halas. When the Bears played at Kezar, he would parade up and down the sidelines, often running onto the field into the arms of the referee.

During a game at Kezar in 1957, McElhenny had just run out of bounds after a short gain, and Halas kicked him right in his rear end. The "King" was outraged, to put it mildly, that he was embarrassed by Halas. Papa Bear was yelling and swearing at the 49ers' players the entire game. He just could not accept that his team was losing to the 49ers. It wasn't the game that was so memorable, but watching Halas having temper tantrums was.

42

The 5th Quarter

TWA's (Trans World Airlines) DC-4 (four engines, propeller-driven) was well regarded by Tony Morabito as his airline of choice for his players in the 1950s. The aircraft became known as the "Morabito's Silverliner," followed by United's DC-6B, as well as the DC-7, until the end of the decade.

When the 49ers traveled to play at Washington on November 13, 1955, the team made its debut in their new road white jerseys—with the shadow numerals (scarlet with black trim)—for the first time in a league game. After the Redskins upset the 49ers 7-0, the players voted unanimously not to wear the road jerseys the rest of the season.

During the decade, owner Tony Morabito made sure his players had the finest of accommodations available for road games: the Riverside Inn (Cambridge), Stevens Hotel and Sheraton Hotel (Chicago), Sheraton Belvedere Hotel (Baltimore), Statler Hotel (Cleveland), Ambassador Hotel (Milwaukee), Sheraton-Town House

Hotel (Los Angeles), Fort Shelby Hotel (Detroit), and the Statler Hotel and Bear Mountain Inn (New York).

Y. A. Tittle, playing left cornerback on defense for his college team, Louisiana State, intercepted a pass against Ole Miss on November 1, 1947, but not before a Rebel grabbed his belt and yanked it hard enough to break the buckle. Tittle, holding the ball with one hand and his pants with the other, returned the interception for nearly 50 yards, as his pants fell to his knees, and he fell flat on his face, 10 yards away from the winning touchdown. LSU lost the game 20-18.

The "Million Dollar Backfield" nickname was first used in the NFL to describe the offensive attack of the Chicago Cardinals in 1947. After an unprecedented amount of money spent by owner Charles Bidwell to lure several of the day's top players to the team—a lineup of halfbacks Paul Christman and Charley Trippi, fullback Paul Harder, and quarterback Marshall Goldberg—he also referred to them separately, as all members of his dream backfield.

In 1954, the nickname "Million Dollar Backfield" was again used to describe the backfield of the 49ers, which produced four Hall of Famers: Tittle, Perry, McElhenny and Johnson. Although, the combined salaries of the foursome were less than $70,000 per season (1954-56).

Flying A (Tidewater Associated Oil Co.) was the official sponsor of the Kezar Stadium scoreboards and the public address system. KYA and KSFO radio stations broadcasted the 49ers' games from the press box on the south side of the playing field. ACME, Goebol, Burgermeister and Falstaff Brewing companies were the team's radio and TV sponsors.

KPIX network first televised the 49ers' road games in glorious black and white throughout the decade. All home games were blacked out within a 150-mile radius. "Bud" Foster, Roy Story and Lon Simmons did the radio broadcasting, while Bob Fouts did the TV commentaries.

The 49ers jumped off to a blazing start in 1954, putting together an 11-game winning streak. They won all six of their preseason games and four straight league games that included a tie to open the regular season. Tittle, Perry and McElhenny all missed action with different injuries, as the team finished the season with a 7-4-1 record.

At the request of the 49ers' GM Lou Spadia, the 49ers' Goal Rushers Booster Club was formed in 1953. At first, it had 1,000 members, and by the end of the decade there were eight chapters and 3,200 members in the Bay Area. The San Francisco chapter held weekly meetings at the Fairmont Hotel, and Clementine, the mascot burro, was an honorary member of the San Francisco Goal Rushers.

43

Making Do

The average 49ers' salary in the early 1950s was less than $6,000 per season. Players needed supplementary income or a chance to further their education in the off-season. Gordy Soltau, representing the 49ers when the NFL Players Association was formed in 1954, demanded a league minimum for the players, but that fell on deaf ears.

Being a student appeared to be the most popular occupation for players during the off-season in the Golden Age, as the players leaned towards getting their bachelor of arts, bachelor of science, master of arts, or Ph.D. degrees.

Some of the players who continued their education in the off-season:

Joe Perry, FB, took classes in public speaking at the University of California Extension in San Francisco, while working his own two-hour nightly radio show on KLX as a disc jockey in Oakland. He also was involved in advertising with Perry Weltner Pontiac in San Francisco.

Bill Jessup, E, took advanced administration courses at Long Beach State and worked part-time at the Long Beach Recreation Department.

Maury Duncan, QB, pursued his degree at San Francisco State and parked cars at the Union Square Garage in San Francisco.

Stan Sheriff, LB, continued his college education towards a master's degree in physical education at Cal Poly.

Gene Babb, FB, continued to sell his paintings, while pursuing his art studies at Austin College in Sherman, Texas.

Bobby Holiday, HB, continued his education in ministry in Dallas, Texas.

Jim Ridlon, DB, worked toward his master's degree at San Francisco State.

C. R. Roberts, FB, continued his college education toward his master of arts degree in business administration at the University of Southern California.

Matt Hazeltine, LB, pursued his college education at the University of California and worked as an insurance broker in Palo Alto, CA.

George Maderos, DB, continued his college education at Chico State and taught math at a high school in North Sacramento.

J. D. Smith, RB, continued to pursue his degree from the University of Chicago, Ill.

**49ers' players who held a part-time job
to supplement their income:**

Dickey Moegle, HB, worked as a mechanical engineer trainee with the Cameron Iron Works at Herrin Transport Co. in Houston, Texas. He also was the manager of the Tidelands Inn, Houston, Texas.

Jerry Mertens, DB, was a familiar figure to ranchers and farmers between San Francisco and Eureka, as he voiced the merits concerning fertilizer products. He worked for Balfour-Guthrie Importers and Exporters.

Hugh McElhenny, HB, worked for Granny Goose Potato Chips as a merchandising and promotional expert. After eight years on the job, he decided to go into the construction business as a partner in Viking Construction Co. in Los Altos, CA.

Gordy Soltau, E, worked for KQED, Channel 9, in San Francisco and KNBC radio in San Francisco. He also worked in sales for Schwabacher-Frey Co., and he was also the player/manager of the 49ers' basketball team.

Bob St. Clair, T, worked as a public relations representative for San Francisco Brewery Corporation, extolling Burgermeister beer from Fresno to Reno, Nevada. At the end of the decade, he opened a liquor store in the Westlake Shopping Center, while playing for the 49ers.

Ted Connolly, G, worked as a sales director for the Heidt Equipment Co. He also worked in public relations for Falstaff Brewing Co. and dabbled in real estate with the John M. Grubb Co. of Oakland, CA.

Joe Arenas, HB, worked construction work and in sales promotion for Schilling Coffee Company in San Francisco.

Leo Nomellini, T, wrestled professionally, making human pretzels out of the Sharp Brothers, earning more money than his football paycheck.

Carroll Hardy, RB, sold Mercurys and Lincolns in Palo Alto and played baseball in the Cleveland Indian farm system.

Y. A. Tittle, QB, worked as a general insurance broker in Palo Alto with the Tittle-Iverson Co. and managed a boys' camp in Napa Valley.

Bobby Hantla, G, and Bud Laughlin, FB, worked for the American United Life Insurance Co. in Kansas City, MO.

Bob Toneff, T, and Marion Campbell, T, worked in construction business on the Peninsula, laboring for a brick contractor.

Frank Morze, C, worked for E. H. Bean Co. in Redwood City, specializing in the selling of industrial cranes.

Rex Berry, DB, worked as a junior power and fuel engineer, with Columbia-Geneva Division of U.S. Steel in Provo, Utah.

Bruno Banducci, G, and Frankie Albert, QB, worked for Rector Motor Co., selling Cadillacs and Oldsmobiles in Burlingame.

Bruce Bosely, G, worked as a health instructor at the Golden Gate Health Studio in San Francisco.

Abe Woodson, DB, worked as an apprentice plumber in the Bay Area.

John Brodie, QB, spent his off-seasons playing on the PGA professional golf circuit.

Clyde Conner, E, worked with the Salvage Transportation Co. in Richmond, CA.

Ed Henke, DE, worked as a sales manager for Di Salvo Trucking Corporation.

Ed Sharkey, G, worked as a watermelon farmer in Arcadia, FL.

Charley Powell, DE, continued his professional boxing career in the off-season.

Al Carapella, T, did "clean-up" work, with New Fangles Window Service company.

Paul Carr, LB, worked in sales with Oshman's Sporting Goods in Houston, TX.

Billy Wilson, E, worked at Leonard's Sports Shop in San Jose, CA.

Clancy Osborne, LB, worked in Ketchican, Alaska, with the Ketchican Pulp Co.

Clay Matthews, DE, worked in the engineering department of Litton Industries in San Carlos, CA.

Monte Clark, T, worked as an automobile salesman for Arta Pontiac in San Francisco.

Harry Babcock, HB, worked for Johnson and Mapes Construction Company.

Bobby Luna, E, sold automobiles in Tuscaloosa, AL.

44

Clementine

"To our ball club, Clementine was more valuable than a chariot horse," said GM Lou Spadia of the 49ers. "She was our lucky charm and an inspiration to the team."

The shaggy, gray-and-white prospectors' burro, represented the idea of the gold miners in the 1869 Gold Rush. From 1954 to 1967, the four-foot, 160-pound burro draped with a red wool blanket, inscribed CLEMENTINE, was the 49ers' mascot for 13 years.

She was a very friendly sort who followed her master obediently down the sidelines at Kezar, bending her head in the direction of an imaginary dandelion, or lifting her head toward the crowd when she heard cheering or booing sounds.

"When I was six years old," said Jan Jeffers of her father, James Lawson, "he acquired the 49er's mascot burro from a neighbor, Dan Custer, who had trained her. Clementine was raised on our ranch in Woodside, California. We would take her to the home games at Kezar Stadium in San Francisco in exchange for complimentary game tickets.

"We were able to park in the west tunnel leading to the field— great parking for sure. I would walk Clementine around the running track when they made a touchdown and have her bow to the audience. I could imagine how Clementine must have felt for once-a-week travel from bucolic country life to a raucous stadium.

"She knew quite a few tricks, like kicking up her heels, when the 49ers scored a touchdown. We also had the opportunity to sit on the 49ers' bench with Y. A. Tittle and Leo Nomellini.

"After my father passed away, I would take her to the games myself when I was just 16. After I turned 18, my interest changed, and I didn't have time to take her to the games."

"Does the donkey trot?" asked assistant coach, Frankie Albert, on behalf of the 49ers' Fan Club. "Most certainly not!" answered her master. "At least she won't cost us a 15-yard penalty," said the facetious Albert.

In 1955, the 49ers struggled all season long, while losing eight games. This caused one disgruntled 49ers fan to suggest, "If the team switched the donkey from team mascot to team member, maybe she'll kick a yard field goal for us, and we'll start winning, and move up in the standings!"

"Jokingly, a 'For Sale' sign was put on Clementine," said Jeffers, "because the 49ers were playing so poorly that year. So we did that.

"When I got to the stadium and walked her around, of course, the news media took photos of the donkey and wrote up an article in the newspaper about how poorly the team was doing. It was a joke, of course, but the front office, particularly GM Lou Spadia, was not happy about that and sent someone down to the field and told us to 'knock it off,' and we did."

Clementine was also a celebrity away from the confines of Kezar. In 1954, during a 49ers-Steelers exhibition game played in Tucson, Arizona, Howard Pyle, then the Governor of Arizona, personally invited the burro to attend the game as an honorary guest. She made the trip and was treated royally with hay, bread, peppermints and ginger biscuits.

The burro also appeared in various parades, private parties, and was one of the performers, in a modern version of the Christmas story that a high school group presented at a Methodist church in San Francisco. One Irish Day parade, which was always held on Market Street, Clementine broke loose from her master. She was found a mile away at 4th and Folsom Street, dehydrated and bruised.

After more than a decade of service parading the sidelines at Kezar in front of her admirers, Clementine passed away on May 30, 1968, at the age of 25. Rumor has it, but it has never been confirmed, that because of the popularity of Clementine, she was the inspiration for the Disney movie, Gus. The movie starred famed actor Don Knotts and a mule (Gus) that was recruited to kick field goals, while crooks attempted to kidnap the mule.

45

The 49ers' Band

Organized under the leadership of Joe McTigue, the 43-piece 49ers' band played at all the 49ers' home games at Kezar during the 1950s, as it was only one of three marching bands in pro football at the time. Many of the members were orchestra leaders and many were outstanding jazz musicians. Most of them worked regularly in local hotels and night clubs and belonged to Local 6, Musician's Union.

McTigue was an executive at United Parcel Service in San Francisco, but devoted his evenings and weekends as the band's director on the field, wearing a white suit. The band played on a bandstand in the corner of the southwest end zone during the season.

"Joe would come to our home every week to meet with my father, Robert Olmstead, who was the entertainment director from 1948-72, before I took over," said Michael Olmstead. "They would work on the band arrangements and charting for the upcoming game, so that my father could choreograph the routines for the 49ers' Majorettes, the first female performing group of its time.

Their halftime performances incorporated a variety of props, and they became a prototype for today's dance/drill teams. I sat next to them and never missed a performance from 1954 to 1967 before I left for college."

The band could be a rowdy group in their own right. During one on-field brawl between the 49ers and the Bears, former boxer Charlie Powell was duking it out in the end zone with a Bears' player, and the band members jumped into the fray, pulling their army belts off their pants to use as weapons.

In the beginning, the band all wore authentic gold miner garb of the Gold Rush days—Western hats, pistol belt and boots.

On the front line, the marching band had 16 trumpets, followed by 10 trombones, 6 clarinets, 5 saxophones, 4 banjos, and 2 drummers.

They played a lot of Dixieland ragtime jazz. Tunes that come to mind are "When the Saints Come Marching In," "South Ramparts Street Parade," "The Victory March," and the stirring "Sweet Georgia Brown," a fans' favorite.

"We were a lively band, and we played at full throttle as we usually had too much to drink, but we had a wonderful time," said a jovial Stu "Skip" Paxon, widely regarded as one of the finest trumpeters in the band.

"You could not watch a game without feeling the beat of our band. After games, win or lose, we played for about 500 enthusiastic folks clapping and giving us ovations on the field. After a few years, we added a more fusion sound that would accommodate the introduction of the 49ers' cheerleaders."

On August 17, 1952, the official 49ers' fight song, "Victory Polka" made its debut at the 49ers-Redskins preseason game at Kezar. The song was written by Martin Judnich, and it was played by Joe McTigue's 49ers' band.

Judnich, a native San Franciscan, was a nationally ranked handball player and an amateur composer. He said he got the inspiration for the song in 1949, when he witnessed a 49ers' game against the Yankees in the old AAFC. The 49ers were trailing early in the game and their rapid fans started a chant of "Go…Go…Go!" The urging from the stands encouraged Martin to build the song around the chorus:

"Let's sing the for For-ty Nin-ers' fight song.
While we chant GO GO GO!
We cheer the team of San Fran-cis-co,
While they GO GO GO GO!
Our gang shall drive and keep on roll-ing,
And across the goal they'll go.
Let's sing the For-ty Nin-ers' fight song,
While we shout GO GO GO GO!"

McTigue said he had received approximately 20 fight songs submitted before Judnich presented him with his composition. He felt it was the first song to catch the spirit and fire of the 49ers' players and fans, and soon after, it was incorporated as part of the band repertoire. Within a few weeks, music sheets were available for sale to the public, and it became a big seller.

46

The Majorettes

I had the pleasure to interview Deanna (O'Mara) Cope, who was a former member from the 14 original San Francisco 49ers Majorettes Corps in the 1950s, who performed at Kezar. Here is the transcript from our interview:

MARTIN JACOBS: What age group were the Majorettes?

DEANNA O'MARA COPE: The majority of the girls were in high school, but sometimes a few eighth graders were included. If I remember correctly, it was 12 or 13 to qualify, as a Senior Corps member and height was around five foot one or five foot two. Many of the girls retired when they graduated high school, but occasionally, someone would stay with the Corps into their late teens or early twenties.

MJ: Were they paid to perform at 49ers' games?

DOC: Robert Olmstead, the 49ers' entertainment director who organized and trained us, had the contract with the 49ers. We, as individuals, did not and were not paid.

MJ: When did the Majorettes practice?

DOC: We practiced on Saturdays for a three-hour rehearsal at the Veteran's Hall in East Palo Alto—both inside and using the streets nearby. I remember a few practices being held at Menlo College, when some of the 49ers' players were also there for practice. Before big shows, we sometimes had additional practices in the evenings in other parts of the Bay Area. I recall being at parks and also at National Guard facilities.

Every summer, we attended summer camps in the Santa Cruz Mountains, where many of the new routines for the coming season were created. The length of rehearsal varied depending on upcoming events, as we might be practicing for a game or parade or working on new routines for appearances in the future.

MJ: How were the Majorettes chosen and when did they first appear at the games?

DOC: The Majorette Corps were organized in 1950, but we began as an organized group at Kezar in 1953. Since then, the Majorettes performed at all 49ers' games throughout the decade and even further. The girls who marched were the best out of several hundred students at the Olmstead schools and were chosen to perform at the 49ers' games. Solo twirlers began performing in 1948, as the Corps were formed several years later.

MJ: Were there tryouts?

DOC: Yes, there were twirling ability requirements. It is my understanding that it became more difficult to qualify for the Corps in later years, once the Corps were recognized on a national level. In addition to twirling batons, some of our novelty numbers included performing with flags, pom-poms, umbrellas, ropes and drums. We also had a few of the Corps' members try their hand at cheerleading.

We would change from our twirling uniforms into what would now be considered very conservative costumes and then go around the track during the game with our pom-poms.

It is my understanding that the Dallas Cowboys claim to have the first NFL cheerleading squad. I have pictures from December 1955 and September 1958, showing that the 49ers did it first!

MJ: Who supplied the uniforms?

DOC: My mother was a beautiful seamstress and made mine and my sister's. I believe the material was provided by the Olmsteads.

MJ: Did the Majorettes perform at away games?

DOC: The Senior Corps performed at some away games. We went to Los Angeles for the Rams-49ers' games; one season, the game was held over the three-day Veteran's Day weekend, meaning we didn't have to miss any school. We went by bus and stopped at a high school field in the Bakersfield area to practice. In 1957, the Majorettes received a tremendous ovation from over 102,000 fans at the game. When the Junior Corps were added, they did not perform at every game, but they did several home games.

When Disneyland opened in 1955, we would perform at the game and then we would leave immediately after the halftime show. At Disneyland, we would march down Main Street, performing with the Disney band. We received free entrance to the park in exchange for performing.

MJ: Who trained the Majorettes?

DOC: As the Corps grew, a few of us, myself included, became teachers at the Olmstead Studios and summer camps. Several of us also taught at a summer camp in Oregon. Mr. Olmstead provided solo twirlers he trained for the games from the time the team was formed.

MJ: Did the Majorettes perform before the game and at halftime?

DOC: Yes, the Corps members did both a pregame and halftime performance. My scrapbook hunting provided the following: "They performed before several million spectators, at nine professional football games, over 50 university, college and high school games, 11 twirling contests, 15 parades and several hundred talent shows, fairs, rodeos, TV broadcasts and basketball games. A total of 88 trophies, including 51 first place and sweepstakes awards were won by the Senior 49er twirlers in 1953."

MJ: How were the Majorettes introduced over the public address system at the games?

DOC: A 1957 49ers' halftime introduction would include the following: "Last year in addition to presenting 12 pregame and halftime shows at Kezar and college games, they appeared on four national TV broadcasts and twirled at the Los Angeles Coliseum and Disneyland.

During the school year, the 64 members of the Majorettes attend 19 Bay Area high schools, and they practice each week in Palo Alto. They also attend a two weeks' summer camp in the Santa Cruz Mountains, where many of the 27 numbers in the unit's repertoire are rehearsed between swimming, hiking, and other camp activities."

MJ: I recalled the Majorettes performing at halftime in the rain and did a performance in the mud at Kezar. Do you recall any of them?

DOC: The Corps actually practiced for potential rainy days in advance. We also had clear vinyl raincoats that went over our uniforms. Over the years, more than one of us fell in the mud while performing. San Francisco Chronicle columnist Herb Caen wrote about our Corps in his column.

MJ: Did the Majorettes perform in the off-season?

DOC: In the off season, the Olmstead Studios had a drum corps, and we marched in parades, mostly in Northern California. We also performed at various other events—that is, when an around-the-world cruise ship came into San Francisco port, we performed on the dock.

We also performed at a car show presenting the next year's models for auto dealerships and on the Santa Cruz Boardwalk. Again, free rides in exchange for performing. A few Corps' members traveled to military bases with the Sixth Army Special Services group. I spent most of the summer after I graduated high school doing that.

When the Globetrotters came to the Bay Area in 1958, they played some of the 49ers' players in basketball games. We performed during halftime at games on February 6, 7, 8 and 9, in 1958. Abe Saperstein bought me lunch on one of those days. One of our solo twirlers traveled in Europe with the Globetrotters, and another traveled with the team in Australia.

MJ: Did the Majorettes perform with the 49ers' band?

DOC: Yes, we marched in front of the band for the pregame show. The majority of the band members were older than the girls in the Corps, but we did sit with them in the end zone. I don't recall knowing any of them, except for Joe McTigue, the band director.

MJ: Did your Majorettes have a common cheer?

DOC: I don't recall the exact cheers, however, we did make up our own 49er Majorettes song on our way to Los Angeles one year, and we shouted it at the top of our lungs, over and over again, while riding on our "49er bus." It went something like this:

"Oh, the Forty Niners are we
And, we're so proud to be
The majorettes for the football team
Cause they're the best you see
Oh, the Forty Niners say
We'll win this game today
The fans will root, the team will play
And, we'll be on our way—Hey!"

MJ: Did you have to make your own travel plans to get to the games?

DOC: We met at a bus station in Palo Alto and took a bus from there. Upon arrival at Kezar, the bus went into the tunnel and remained there throughout the game. We shared the tunnel with Clementine, so we did get to pet her and occasionally feed her.

MJ: Did you ever have a chance to mingle with the players?

DOC: Because of our game day practice schedule versus the team's warm-up/playing schedule, we did not get a chance to mingle with them while at Kezar. I did meet a few of the players on other occasions. At the end our first season in the Corps, Leo Nomellini came to one of our practices and presented each of us with a trophy, thanking us for our participation at games. In 1956, there was a "meet and greet" type event called "Rancho Roundup" at Town and Country

Village in Palo Alto. There, we performed while Ed Henke, Y. A. Tittle and Hugh McElhenny were signing autographs.

Early in his career, Bob St. Clair was at practice at Menlo College, and a photo was taken with his arms outstretched, with some of the twirlers in front of him to show just how wide his arm span was. I'm not sure if the photographer was with a local newspaper or from the 49ers, but I have never seen the picture. That same day, there was also a radio interview done with St. Clair for broadcast at a later date. I was involved in a few minutes of that interview, talking about our Corps' practices and summer camp.

47

The Kezar Vendor

Mr. Bruce Lombardi, a native San Franciscan now residing in Arizona, is a throwback vendor from the Kezar era. Here are some excerpts from a transcript of our interview:

MARTIN JACOBS: How did you hear about vending?

BRUCE LOMBARDI: My dad had a teamster friend, who vended part-time at Kezar. A lot of vendors in those days were teamsters, or truck drivers, who vended on the side for extra money. My dad's friend was selling programs outside the stadium, and he asked him if he could get me into the game.

This was my very first time I was at Kezar, as he gave me 10 programs and told me to go inside and sell them, which I did. When I was done, I gave him the money. He didn't pay me anything, but he said I got inside, "so go watch the game."

At the time, I only cared about watching a 49ers' game, but the following week, I went back to Kezar, and I stood in a long line with about 40 other kids, wanting to vend at the game.

There was this guy who was in charge of picking the vendors to work. Not everyone got picked. It was based on the projected crowd.

That morning, my dad, a reserve police officer, was in his uniform and stood behind me in line. When the guy picking the kids took a look at my dad, he pointed me out, and I got picked to go in and sell. I was just 12 at the time, but I turned 13 by mid-season.

MJ: So your Dad also worked at the games?

BL: Yes, the S.F.P.D. had a whole department of reserves back then. They didn't get paid. He worked security detail before and after the games, and he helped direct traffic. During the games, he was on the field, usually behind the players' bench. He was there to be sure that no crazy fans came down from the stands or onto the field. If they did, he would bust them. There was a paddy wagon always ready, just in case.

MJ: Were you issued a vendor's uniform?

BL: They gave me a hat of some sort and a numbered badge. I had to buy an apron and a money changer, which I still have. Other than that, I just wore our regular street clothes at the game.

MJ: How many hours a game did you put in vending?

BL: I usually arrived at the stadium about 8 a.m. and stood outside until the boss came out. He picked his crew for the day and then I went inside to work.

I would start walking the aisles about 11:00. The games started at 1 p.m., and I would sell until midway through the fourth quarter. Considering I started working about four hours before the game, it was a long day. After the game, I usually waited for my dad to finish directing traffic. Once most of the traffic was gone, we would head home.

MJ: What did you sell?

In my case, it was soda. The procedure was the boss gave us a batch of tickets. There were two tickets attached together; I tore off one and I gave the other ticket to the boss to get a load of soda. I would keep the other ticket. One load consisted of a double tray of, I believe, 16 sodas in this metal tray.

I was not very big then, maybe 120 pounds, and it was very heavy and sticky, as they were supposed to heat-seal the lids on the sodas, but the lids always came off. I sold Cokes, 7-UPs and orange sodas. Nobody ever wanted the orange drinks. Then I'd walk up and down the aisles while the sodas would splash around, and I ended up with all this soda in my metal tray. At the end of the day, I counted the number of tickets I had left, and that showed me how many loads I sold.

MJ: Did you always sell soda?

BL: Only my first season, because I was one the youngest and the newest kid. My second season I was working every game, but I didn't sell soda anymore. Somehow, I was introduced to this guy running a souvenir stand, and I told him I would love to sell souvenirs.

At the time, he had only one other old guy selling the stuff. In fact, it is hard to believe it today, but back then, there was only one guy walking around, carrying just pennants.

So, the guy with the souvenir stand gave me a small card table that I set up by one of the gates for when the fans started coming into the stadium. Once the game started, I would close it up and take my table with my basket with hats, pennants, pins and some other stuff, and I would set up at halftime near a concession stand and again at the end of the game near an exit.

I started making $25 to $35 dollars a game, and I loved it. From then on I was hooked, because I had friends delivering newspapers every day, and they were making less than I did for one day's work.

In between selling souvenirs, I sold hot dogs, and when I turned 21, I sold beer. I made good money in those days. I vended through Kezar's last season of 1970. Then we moved to Candlestick. I really didn't want the team to move, because I lived so close by Kezar.

MJ: How were you paid?

BL: We made 20 percent of whatever we sold, in cash. If I was short, because I made a mistake, I paid for it. If I got tips, that would add to the total I got to keep.

MJ: Did you have to join a union?

BL: Not at first, because as a kid, I got a Junior work permit. But when I became 18, I joined the 468 Vendor's Union, and I had to pay union dues.

MJ: How were the working conditions at Kezar?

BL: I remember our boss telling us the 49ers were getting complaints from the City, that our fans were critical of our vending and concessions procedures, like cold hot dogs and warm sodas. Well, the 49ers told the City, who they rented the stadium from, which was based on the paid attendance, that the they had no jurisdiction whatsoever in the matter the way the vendors did their job. Nothing really changed.

MJ: Did you personally receive any complaints?

BL: One game I was selling hot dogs. This is in the day when I had to put the hot dogs together with the bun and mustard. I had a container filled with hot water with the dogs in it, and on the side of it, we kept the mustard and napkins. The mustard had an open container, so I was walking down the steps and my strap broke off my shoulder holding the container, and the whole container starts tumbling down the steps with the mustard, including the large bills I kept under the container, and everything went flying.

Some guy sitting about three rows down got spattered with the mustard. Poor fellow. It went all over his face, his cream-colored jacket and pants. I caught some heat from him, as well as from my boss. I lost about $20 to $30 in the accident.

MJ: Did you ever get a chance to encounter any celebrities or players?

I do remember selling a hot dog to Bing Crosby. The funny thing was that I remember he was grumpy. Not friendly at all. I always remembered that. By the way, no tip. Also, Dick Lane, the famous television announcer ("Whoa, Nellie!"), Bob Hope and Andy Gillis bought beers from me.

MJ: Any regrets Mr. Lombardi?

BL: Maybe one. It was an unusually warm day at Kezar, and we were having our way with the Rams—something like 34-0. I mean we were pounding them! It was the first season I was selling beer. When I finished a load, I usually would run back to check out to another one, but I was so excited, I started drinking the beers. After the second or third case, I passed out, and I couldn't last the whole game. I was done by halftime. The next day I had such a hangover.

48

49ers' Gear

When the 49ers played in the AAFC from 1946-49, their team jerseys were just seen as part of a team's regular equipment. They lacked appeal and had no fancy embellishments. "We regarded them as work clothes, in the same way a house painter wears overalls," said quarterback, Frankie Albert.

(Author's Note: From 1946-47, the team color jersey was cardinal; beginning in 1948, the team changed to scarlet.)

In 1950, when the 49ers joined the NFL, the team's first issued jersey was referred to as a "warm-weather" jersey, made of cotton, stretch, durene yarn, with added sewn elbow pockets, reinforced shoulders, and an extended button-down flap crotch piece (if a player desired), much like their 1948-49 equivalent, except three white parallel (3/4 -inch x 3/4-inch x 3/4-inch) stripes were added to the sleeves.

The jersey was scarlet in color with eight-inch, sewn, white numbers on front and 10-inch numbers on the back, with long sleeves. For road games, the color scheme was reversed using a white, durene jersey.

A manufacturer's label was either sewn in the collar or at the bottom front of the jersey with an added fly tag to indicate the size.

The label specified the supplier's name and sometimes washing instructions. Known suppliers during the decade were King O'Shea and Wilson Sporting Equipment (Chicago).

Each player was issued one home and one away jersey for the entire season; thus, the need for repairs was in abundance. It wasn't uncommon for a jersey to have upwards of 20-25 sewn repairs during a season, in which 49ers' trainers repaired them right on the sidelines at halftime, using needle and thread or duct tape. Most of the jerseys did not survive beyond the season, and then they had to be replaced.

In 1955, the team added another jersey, same style, to the line to be used basically for colder weather. It was a heavier cotton durene blend. Furthermore, an experimental lighter rayon/cotton blend "tear-away" material jersey was also introduced for the warmer climate. The tear-away jersey was discarded after only one season.

For the 1957 and 1958 seasons, small white four-inch block numerals (or TV numbers) were added to the upper sleeves. Although, in 1959 they added an inch to the size of the numerals.

The uniform pants were made of a shiny, satin material on front, and on the back, a stretch nylon material with built-in pockets for knee pads. Belt loops were attached and black belts were issued by the team. The team also changed the garment color of the pants three times—silver, white and gold—during the decade.

The earliest 49ers' helmets were made of leather with little padding. The helmets would be better described as head coverings with little effect in softening blows to the head. By the 1950s, helmets began undergoing significant improvements and offered some relief from head and facial injuries, with additional padding and face protectors.

During the decade, the 49ers used various suppliers for their game helmets—Riddell, Wilson and Rawlings. Many players were under contract with athletic suppliers, and they had an option to use whatever style and supplier they chose. Bob St. Clair and John Henry Johnson wore a Wilson leather helmet during their tenure with the 49ers, whereas running back Hugh McElhenny wore a leather Wilson helmet in his 1952 inaugural season, and then switched over to a Riddell RT-2 plastic Tenite, six-loop 12-point suspension helmet in 1953.

The RT-2 helmet was manufactured in two halves that were joined and reinforced by a piece of extruded Tenite. Riddell upgraded this product in late 1954, introducing the RK-4 model. This employed the same shell mold as the RT-2 but used a different plastic.

In 1955, Riddell introduced a one-piece plastic helmet. The "Tru-Kurv" or TK-5, with a six-point suspension webbing, was introduced in 1959.

It is unclear why the 49ers changed the color of their helmets as often as they did.

Beginning in 1950, the 49ers wore solid silver helmets until 1952, when they changed to scarlet helmets with a single silver center stripe that were used from 1953-55. In 1956, they wore a solid white helmet.

For the 1957-58 season, they wore solid gold helmets, and in 1959, a silver helmet was introduced with three red center stripes added. The color of the paint was referenced by a number code, according to Riddell Corporation, who painted over the gray helmet shells.

In 1953, protective face guards were added to the helmets. Players like Hardy Brown, Art Michalik, Doug Hogland, Leo Nomellini and Clay Matthews, started wearing clear Lucite face masks.

Although generically called "acrylic safety glass," Lucite was not considered safe for use as a football face mask. When it broke, it did so in dagger-like pieces that could cause more harm than the blunt force trauma the material was supposed to absorb.

Ironically, in a preseason game in 1954, Joe Perry suffered a jaw injury and needed some protection placed over his face. At halftime, a Lucite protective cover was placed on the helmet to protect the jawbone, and Perry was able to continue playing the game.

Before the decade was over, the NFL would ban Lucite masks. Also in 1954, the NFL made it mandatory that all players wear some type of face protection. Within that decision was the provision that players already in the league could continue to play without a mask, if they chose to do so.

A new mask was introduced and took the form of a rubber-coated steel tube shaped in a semicircle that was bolted to each side of a helmet, just below the ear holes. This mask was commonly called the "single-bar" face mask.

Still, the interior lineman and linebackers requested more protection. Upon their requests, Riddell took the single-bar mask and added a vertical bar attached at the midpoint that bowed out slightly in an upward direction, before arcing back to a part of the helmet, just above a player's nose.

A third component, an ellipse, attached below the horizontal bar. Turned upside down, the mask looked like a line drawing of an umbrella. This style became standard model for the blockers and defenders the rest of the decade.

Sideline jackets were issued to all 49ers' team members. They were made from a red canvas whipcord material, with matching stretch ribbed knit waistbands, cuffs, and collars, with three silver stripes added, and snap-on buttons on the front. The inside lining was made of satin fabric. The words "Forty Niners" was sewn in script style on the back of the jacket in tackle-twill lettering.

In 1959, block letters replaced the script style lettering. The jacket itself was manufactured by King O'Shea. A supplier's label was sewn in the collar, and underneath the label a one-inch felt swatch with the player's number was affixed inside the collar. At the very bottom of the back of the jacket, a fly tag was sewn inside the lining of the jacket, specifying the size.

The sideline capes were not issued to any particular player but were used by numerous team members during a season. The outer shell lining was of a shiny satin material with snap-on buttons, a hood with a zipper, slash pockets, and an inner heavy fur lining for cold and rainy weather.

A sewn fly tag indicating the size was attached to either a King O'Shea or Wilson Athletic Equipment label. On the back of the cape were large size tackle twill sewn, five-inch satin silver or gold block letters that spelled "FORTY NINERS." From 1950-56, the cape's traditional colors were scarlet with white stripes. The team changed their cape's colors to scarlet and gold for the 1957-58 season, but in 1959, they went to scarlet again but with silver stripes.

In honor of the late New York Giants' owner, Wellington Mara, one of the most beloved and respected figures in professional sports history, the official football of the NFL was called "The Duke" at the suggestion of Chicago Bear's owner George Halas. Every throw, every kick, every touchdown and every point in every NFL game was made with a Wilson football.

The NFL footballs used in the 1950s were produced only by Wilson Sporting Goods Company and became the league's official supplier of game balls. Called the "pigskin," it was not made of pigskin at all but cowhide. All balls were made by hand and made of top leather, handsewn, lockstitch seams.

During the Golden Age, dark leather balls were used for afternoon games, and white-painted leather ones were used for night games. In

1956, the white balls were replaced with a standard daytime football circled by two white stripes.

Advancements in stadium lighting had made night balls unnecessary. And in 1957, a pebble-grained, tan leather football was introduced and designed for a good grip. Each football was stamped... Made by Wilson...Official National Football League...Eastern and Western Conference...Bert Bell Commissioner...Thorp Sporting Good, New York (Distributor)...and The DUKE.

49

Investing in 49ers' Memorabilia

In times of the uncertainty of Wall Street, collecting 49ers' memorabilia continues to be the subject of the whims or vicissitudes of an unstable market place. Still, their prices and values are holding strong and steadily compounding. Like the stock market, collectible pricing is based on perceived value. When the economy's general market seems uncertain, the perceived value of enduring collectibles typically increases, because the consumer can touch, feel and smell what it is they're attaining—unlike stocks and bonds.

This is just one of the reasons why collecting 49ers' memorabilia hold its own during any slowdown in the economy. Another reason the collectible market jumps during recession is due to the collector having control of the materials. They can choose to sell or buy, creating their own collection value. A point to remember is to buy smart and buy quality.

Online stores, catalog auctions, and or private sales continue to flourish. The craze of tangible relics and collectibles, the allure of the collecting hobby, expanding into the mainstream of nostalgia, has continued to stir into a profitable business. It's not only the game-worn garments or the high-energy collector cards, it's the avant-garde generation of participants who continue to stimulate its avocation. The oldies are always the goodies, and they are continuing to command dynamic values.

Personally, I have only witnessed a very slight depreciation in the collectible market. And as long as the quality and provenance of the relics and collectibles are assured, they are still a solid investment.

Quality 49ers' memorabilia always holds a premium, so collect the names of Hall of Famers and players who contributed greatly to the franchise. You can expect to pay a high premium for autographs, signed jerseys and helmets, from any mega stars. Also, it's thrilling to witness lively enthusiasm from collectors at memorabilia and card shows in person.

Lastly, be cautious. To be sure, there are always a pothole or two on the road to building a collection. But more often than not, the general trend of enhancement in the sports memorabilia industry provides security and promises greater rewards than any other financial endeavor. Follow your eye and your heart—this is an exciting and flourishing hobby we're in. Savor your 49ers collectibles, the old and obscure, and their future outlook.

Acquisitions of 49ers' memorabilia is a dynamic and well-seasoned mature investment, and it generally glitters with immensely more radiance than the featureless stock certificate. It's vital when purchasing an item that the dealer is reputable or the person is recognized in the hobby.

There are plenty of fakes out there in the industry, and be sure to ask for a Certificate of Authenticity (COA) that documents the item. One great feature as a collector myself is I can always safely redeem my investment—if I wanted to. It's an exciting way to diversify your portfolio or just to enjoy a route to a cozy retirement.

Although for me, collecting 49ers' memorabilia is not a matter of investing; it's more important than that. Collecting still remains a huge part of my life, and I know many other collectors feel the same way. I asked myself, which items from my collection should be locked away in a vault and buried beneath old Kezar Stadium?

My conclusion was all of them should. I've been collecting since I was nine-years old, and I treasure them for what they represent and what they mean to me personally, and not for what they are worth monetarily. I've experienced through the ages that friends, jobs, relationships, even dreams come and go, but collecting 49ers still remains constant for me.

Epilogue

The 49ers' teams of the Golden Age were perhaps the most adulated and reviled in 49ers history. When the 49ers joined the NFL in 1950, they were a mystery and staggered through a 3-9 season. How could a team that had been so strong, that posssessed runners such as Joe "The Jet" Perry and John Strzykalski, bolstered by All-American rookies Leo "The Lion" Nomellini and the multi-talented receiver Gordy Soltau, and a relentless scrambling quarterback wizard, Frankie Albert, flop so badly? There was no easy answer.

But help came quickly. The 49ers latched onto Hardy "Hatchet" Brown, who became a terror on running backs, using his shoulder as battering ram. Even more important to the future came quarterback Y. A. Tittle with undeniable virtues. His arrival signaled a more lethal attack, and the 49ers rebounded in 1951 with a 7-4-1 record.

Receiver Billy Wilson also broke in with the team in 1951, who would prove to be Tittle's favorite target throughout the decade. He went on to lead the NFL three times in pass receptions (1954, 56-57).

In 1952, the 49ers added more firepower as Hugh McElhenny, an electrifying runner, became an instant sensation and NFL rookie of the year. The offensive line was bolstered by such luminaries as Bill

"Tiger" Johnson at center, alongside Bruno Banducci at guard, and later the 6-foot-9 Bob St. Clair was added at tackle.

From 1952 through 1954, the 49ers led the league in rushing, as Perry became the first NFL runner to rush for more than 1,000 yards in successive seasons (1953-54). The starting backfield in 1954—Tittle, McElhenny, Perry and John Henry Johnson—have all been enshrined in the Pro Football Hall of Fame. Add the quick and elusive Joe Arenas, one of the most elite kick returners in the league to the lineup, and the 49ers had an explosive offense.

Unfortunately, the defense didn't hold up its end. The 49ers did come close to a division title in 1953 with a 9-3 record, but Detroit won out. There were far too many games the 49ers lost due to a mediocre defense. Teams like the Rams, Lions, Bears, Colts and Packers ended up with the division crowns in the decade.

The 49ers rivalry against the Rams were as intense as any in sports. In fact, the largest regular-season crowd in pro football history (102,368) saw the two West Coast rivals battle at the Los Angeles Coliseum in 1957.

With expectations high in 1955, their first-ever head coach "Buck" Shaw was replaced by a displinarian coach in Norm "Red" Strader who was never popular with the players. That season, a foot injury limited McElhenny to minimul use; Tittle and John Henry Johnson also became casualties and the 49ers finished 4-8. Strader was fired after just one season.

Frankie Albert became the 49ers' new head coach. By the end of the 1957 season, the 49ers ended up with an 8-4 record, good enough for a first-place tie with the Lions. Despite the unveiling of the "alley-oop" pass play, where Tittle and receiver R. C. Owens, who used his extrodinary leaping ability to outjump defenders to win five games, the team came up short in a one-game playoff against Detroit, losing 31-27.

The 1957 season was bittersweet as owner Tony Morabito suffered a fatal heart attack in the press box at Kezar. The man whose fortitude had brought the 49ers into being would never live to see his team win a championship.

Albert stepped down after a 6-6 finish in 1958, and Howard "Red" Hickey replaced him. Over the next few seasons, new reliables arrived in the persons of tackle Charlie Krueger, guard Ted Connolly, defensive back and kick returner specialist Abe Woodson, and the emergence of quarterback John Brodie, along with halfback J. D. Smith, would lead the 49ers into the next decade.

Those 49ers' players who adorned the scarlet, silver and gold uniforms during the Golden Age were the original 49ers, the unsung heroes who ended up in the Hall of Fame. Sure, they were never crowned champions, but they became the performers who laid the foundation for the 49ers' championship years to follow.

Acknowledgments

I would like to extend my sincere appreciation to those San Francisco 49ers' players and the families of the deceased players, who generously cooperated to lengthy interviews and shared their fascinating remembrances of their earliest days with the 49ers, on and off the field. Special thanks to Tex Noel, Executive Director of the Intercollegiate Football Researchers Association (IFRA), who enabled me to ascertain and verify many of the facts and statistics in this project, and for his countless hours of hard work that made this book a reality. To Kim Foster and Robert Zingmark for their editorial support on this project, Jack McGuire, Bruce Lombardi, Jan Jeffers, Deana (Mara) Cope, Greg Garr, Michael Olmstead, Elmer Carr, Donnan Sinn, Matt Southard, Frank Rippon, Wilson Sporting Goods Company; Bill Van Niekerken, Library editor of the *San Francisco Chronicle*, *San Francisco Examiner*, *United Press International*, *Associated Press*, and Cal-Pictures archival resources for their photo contributions. And expressly to all those 49ers' Faithful fans who shared their memories of our legendary 49ers during their formative years during the Golden Age of 49ers' football.

Meet the Author

As a writer and collector of 49ers memorabilia for over six decades, Martin S. Jacobs, has established himself in virtually all aspects of the team's 70-year history. His journey began as a youth in the 1950s vending at old Kezar Stadium. During the tumultuous 1970s and into the Super '80s, he operated the "Sports Stop," serving the 49ers' Faithful with team apparel, souvenirs and collectibles. In 2000, Jacobs was bestowed with the honor of being selected the 49ers' No. 1 Fan of the Year by *VISA International*. A plaque of commendation from the 49ers is on display at the NFL Hall of Fame in Canton, Ohio.

In a span covering 50 years, he has covered the 49ers for *Pro Football Weekly, Football Digest, The Sporting News*, Street & Smith's NFL annuals, *Gridiron Greats*, and as "The Collector" in the 49ers' Gameday magazine. He has authored two other books with 49ers historical significance: *Before They Were Champions—The San Francisco 49ers 1958 Season*, and *San Francisco 49ers*—Images of Sport. Also, in 2015, Jacobs was featured by 49ers Studio films in their weekly 49ers' Faithful TV series (No. 7), as the "Throwback."

Today Jacobs resides in San Francisco with his family. He welcomes your comments and he can be reached by email at MJacobs784@aol.com.

CPSIA information can be obtained
at www.ICGtesting.com
Printed in the USA
BVHW041824100121
597498BV00031B/517